Positive Thinking Power of Optimism

Believe in Yourself for Better Living

Gautam Sharma

I0424092

COPYRIGHT

The Essence

"The mind is everything. What we think is what we are and what we become"

from the teachings of Gautama Budha(the Enlightened)

Dedications:

Dear friends across the globe,

This book is dedicated to my wife, Shabnam Sharma whose love, optimism, kindness, energy and support makes me and our family radiantly fulfilled. Thanks to our immediate and extended family and friends located across several countries for diverse and joyful experiences shared over many years. The Universe provides abundance and this is to share with valued readers ,that you are the reason for this book. The Empowerment Series is not about me but about all of you .It is heartening to note that many readers have chosen to empower themselves and others in their circles of influence.

Thanks to the growing number of friendly, helpful people who keep sending feedback and favorable reviews through social and professional networking media and platforms.

Praise for Positive Thinking Power of Optimism.

*This book is potentially transforming

Highly recommended for all.

Vinny M, Melbourne

*A motivating, easy to read book that all of us will appreciate. Gautam   Sharma is an intelligent man who has penned a distilled version of centuries old universal laws and modern research findings. This book will give you very positive vibes and shall certainly give you the confidence to meet challenging situations! Worth reading right away. Herbert D.

*Positive thinking and joyous optimism are the only attitudes that keeps us happy and healthy. Gautam Sharma has aptly steered us to believe in this truth. A very informative,must read book.

* I must compliment Gautam Sharma for sharing with all of us the wisdom of positive thinking. I have really liked when he says "Your thoughts shape your world and that optimism is most important for happiness. Furthermore, optimism is the topmost habit/skill of all successful people". In

fact, the Gallup survey on national leadership rates hope as the top of the pile". Obama became President on this promise! K.T. *What a wonderful way to articulate your perspectives on an all important aspect of life, in the form of this book. Congratulations and wishing Gautam Sharma many more.

S.O.

*Excellent book on empowerment and how it guides our actions. Overall a five Star.

 * "Are you constantly worrying about tomorrow? Are you looking to do away with stress from your life? To get these answers read this book by
 Gautam Sharma and start to enjoy your life..Beautifully written" .. Sheena M

* In this extraordinary book, the author provides fresh insights into the power of positive thinking and how we have an opportunity to shape the outcomes of life's journey. Based on his personal experiences and empirical research studies, the author has drawn inspiration from diverse sources and laid out for his readers, concrete actions to overcome adversities and realize the full potential of personal creativity. An invaluable read !

 Nita..B.

Disclaimer :

The author is sharing his thoughts and philosophy for informational and educational purposes. Advice and recommendations given here are not for treatment for any medical or mental conditions. You are solely responsible for consulting certified medical practitioners for treatment based on your specific situation and needs.

Table of Contents

Introduction

INTRODUCTION

"Expect the Best and the Universe will materialize your goals,dreams and desires" "(from the Scriptures)

"Optimism, hope ,faith can manifest miracles"(translated from the Vedas)
From as early as the Scriptures and the Vedas till the recent 2015 studies,research at top worldwide institutions, findings and writings confirm the universal truth remains ever constant "Your thoughts shape your world and that optimism is most important for happiness. Furthermore, optimism is the topmost habit /skill of all successful people.

This book has been written based on centuries old universal laws as well as modern research findings for improving lives. You can start having faith in yourselves and regain your confidence and self -esteem so as to   achieve your goals. Practice these simple steps several times every day:

A. Trust the Universe: You are part of Divine creation and a magnificent expression of life. Embrace and accept your oneness with Divinity and repeat this in your thoughts and in words upon awakening, during the day and just before going to sleep:" I am one with Divinity and a magnificent expression of divine life. I am meant to be safe,

secure and well in all possible ways at all times."
B. Keep focused on the positive, because whatever
you focus on expands So expand on the positive
about who you are and all that you have. Give
thanks and be grateful for the fact that you are
alive, be thankful that you have enough air to
breathe and since you can breathe, you can smell
the freshness of nature and the roses. Be thankful
for the fact that the sun, air and water keep all
humans, other live forms and vegetation alive. We
all have so many things to be grateful about- the
list would run into dozens or even hundreds and
thousands. With a habit giving thanks and being
grateful, you are increasing the flow of goodness
that you receive. A very simple yet effective
positive affirmation to repeat in your mind is :"I
deserve the best, expect the best and receive the
best right now and at all times". Say the above and
believe that you are all right and that all is well ,
regardless of your present circumstances. Have
ongoing faith in the Universe and you will be
doing all right
There is so much abundance of what the Creator
has granted you and the more you dwell on
abundance and the goodness, the more you will
receive." Conceive, believe and achieve" is not a
mere slogan, it is the foundation for manifesting
positive energy vibrations in the form of material
things Divinity has shaped this law for all living
beings since the dawn of creation for ever.

Thought process is essential for creating our constantly evolving lives. Your thoughts completely give shape to your experiences , your mental state of mind and to all material things you have.

All experiences in our lives are shaped by our thoughts. Originating from the varied background of our thoughts and belief systems, we create everything **towards us which is defined by who**we are and all that we have. Sounds a bit fascinating and somewhat magical doesn't it ? But that's how it works; mainly by thinking of positive outcomes most of the times, we get them to manifest for us. Scientific studies show that for humans to direct our life outcomes, we have to learn to control the nature of our recurring and dominant mental self-talk. Peaceful, harmonious, loving self-talk can be achieved with sustained focus and regular practice to continue drawing only positive events into our lives - all what we intend to have and experience for better living. The power of positive thinking can help you achieve everything,once you accept the truth that your thoughts create your reality,now and into the future. In very practical ways and encouraging terms , we are rightfully the true creators of our own world,every time and under all circumstances. By ourselves, we shape our lives with our thoughts, words, beliefs and feelings. At first glance this logic may perhaps seem false,irrelevant or baseless because some can instantly point to events that were seemingly beyond your control:your birth circumstances, some illnesses, some accidents, your enemies, and that storm or hurricane that killed so many. **Understandably no** one says to themselves: it's okay that I sometimes get harmed, mugged or cheated."To clarify the above, let's get to the core of the universal truth with precision.: long before birth , initially at mostly subconscious levels and subsequently consciously you created them all: every event,all your life experiences to their finest details. Before birth we had chosen the wider pathways,during life we choose the lanes. One perfectly functional, healthy body with millions of arteries

To sum up, your mental patterns define your life profile: genetics,ancestry, continent skin form, body shape , intelligence as well as some predefined milestones like specific family members , a serious setback, a windfall inheritance or newly found fortunes. If only we had all realized it much earlier that thinking habits and patterns were the cause that had so much effect on how our lives will play out. As you get along in life, you continuously choose your arterial pathways every second of your waking lives— with your thinking. Simply put, your thoughts accumulate and become potent beliefs, the strongest ones operating at subconscious levels and affecting your upcoming sequence of life choices. Little wonder that when something unpleasant happens, we wonder why it came about.

By switching on the positive mental state of being, let's us recognize that we are an integral part of the universal magnificence. We are expressions of the highest consciousness and we forget our greatness many times mainly that our dreams and desires can become reality with our thought power being attuned to Divinity. The earlier we realize this truth and take conscious control of our thoughts the earlier we declare our freedom and begin living fulfilled lives

Respond to the call to action , move away from mere existence towards joyous living.

 Start believing that everyone is part of Divinity and truly magnificent., You are one with the ultimate source-the Super consciousness".These are proven values in spirituality for over 3,000 years and will continue remain valid to uplift humanity.

The truth above compliments the laws of contemporary science and metaphysics .Modern scientists, researching about the fundamental building blocks of the universe are discovering other laws. Here's one: both the presence and the behavior of subatomic particles depend on what is going on in the mind of the scientist".

"This may sound a bit fictional make believe but is really scientifically true and has been replicated many times. The implications are stunning. As one expert science researcher put it, "Physicists these days are uncovering untapped frontiers."

Conventional science assumes that consciousness arises from physical objects. Metaphysics states that the reverse is true too, something which Asian Hindu Masters have known for 3,000 years. No wonder that Buddha(the enlightened) put it this way: "All that we are is the result of what we have thought. The mind is everything. What we think is what we are and what we become. The whole world is the projection of our thoughts"
Our belief system is as mysterious as it is complex. We talk about and express ourselves through a set of beliefs which have been ingrained in us since birth ; whatever we firmly believe ,plays out in our experiences some of which are part of our subconscious. problems. If you believe you will lose your faculties as you age, you bring about early aging on yourself. Many others who believe that age is just a number which doesn't slow them down in their physical and mental abilities as years go by, can run a marathon or do well at speed reading and data analytics well over sixty too.

My bet would be that almost every community and the group of irrational elements in their belief systems. (If this is anything irrational another question)

Examples that come to mind, let's see if I can solve almost read each answer.

Software executives who seem to think that the methods of waterfall development can produce sometimes important innovations.

Voters who believe that their individual votes made a difference in the presidential election

Parents who believe their child is unique and special

Investors, they say, the calendar can market or exceeded the average performance through daily transactions.Many mentors,teachers, researchers and most successful people reinstate the statement "Whether you believe you can, or instead you think you can't, either way,you are absolutely right." The Universe s

In the American folklore there is a small but meaningful story among the Mahicans' native American tribe:

A grandfather and his grandson are sitting by a campfire on a cool, silent night , wrapped in warm clothing and gazing into the leaping flames. High on rocky ledges, a wildcat wails menacingly and loudly and another wildcat responds from a distance. Minutes later, the old man pauses between puffs on his pipe and says:

Grandson,:here are two wildcats inside everyone. One is good and the other is bad.

?Who are they, Grand dad ? asks the interested, curious boy.

?They are fighting each other,? says the old , wise man.

The boy considers this, then asks, ?Why are they good and bad??

The good one is your love, your peace and your truth. The bad one is your fear, your anger and your bad habits

The fire crackles and sparks flare all around. The wildcat on the ridge wails again and the grandpa puffs happily on his pipe.

Finally, the boy asks: who will win, grandfather?

Well,says the old man, removing the pipe once more. The one that wins is the one you attend to.

 Attend to the good in you. Connect to the source and you will be provided for.

You become what you think of most. What you feel follows you, what you believe builds around you.

If perhaps you are wondering: if we get what we focus on, why do we get so much of what we don't want? This is because we often focus most passionately on what we don't want, and our personal universe always grants our greatest passions. Be very precise and specific about what you want and do not put thought on what you don't want. Double negatives don't work. So skip the "I don't want to be sick any more" , largely because the word sick sticks out ,so the ideal statement or thought would be " I am radiantly healthy right here and now and for always and can help others because I have perfect health and strength. If you are unhappy with your current job or the profession itself that you are in, steer clear from the thoughts of how you can get away from your horrible workplace. Instead visualize a happy workplace, a productive job which gives you satisfaction and gets you rewards of remuneration and recognition. you Here is the most strongly negative level of manifestation-thought process. Thinking you're not the creator of your life, but a victim of circumstances Blaming your condition on everything other than yourself, maybe the Heavens even your ancestry family, fate birth, parents, country, recession, accidents, sickness or the leaders. It's been always difficult. You are inherently incapable. You are a victim and life is a torment..... Are you this person?

Maybe better and positive at the next level, more evolved: you are sometimes the maker of your own life. You can influence some events, but mostly, external forces are too strong to fight off. You blame most of your condition on something other than yourself. You take some responsibility for what happens to you. You have some value some potential. Life is a struggle with a few highlights..... Are you like this?

Otherwise, let's take it higher:you are largely the maker of your life. You can influence most events, though sometimes external forces are too great. You take responsibility for most of your actions. You spend little time blaming others for painful events. You are a valuable person with faults. You have a lot of potential. Life is an interesting and often enjoyable challenge. Are you closer to this?

Now the highest: at the high standard of evolved level where the belief is that you are entirely the maker of your life. You are part of the great field of consciousness that has many adventures and many realities, including yours. You do not see your earth character as you, but as a spiritual being leading in an evolved human form . Your every thought, attitude and action is your doing You are fully responsible, not only for your creations but for your response to your creations. You never blame or judge others for your experiences. Your inherent worth and value are increasing everyday. Your life is a wonderful, joyful adventure on a smooth pathway, with a few downs but mostly ups all along.

Are you at this stage ?These are standards of belief Whatever standard of manifestation-belief you own you will create the conditions that will prove you right. What you believe will keep happening for you and around you.

Mind manifests miracles the proven universal truth. Believe and accept optimism , happiness, health,love, peace , harmony , joy, fulfillment , self-love and self-worth and experience all of these in abundance once you decide to so empower your life. Growing up, i was scolded by my parents, which many children get to hear:" do not behave as if the whole world revolves around you". In fact, it does. Or rather, my world does. And so does yours. Literally. As quantum physics is beginning to discover, there are an infinite number of energy worlds . Your consciousness experiences revolve around you, creating all that you know and experience and the trillion plus cells in your body and mind. You are the etheric body in an energy bubble of your making. Such energy field interacts with energy fields of others. Every direction you head in with your body, mind and aura, you create events and details of your experiences.

CHAPTER ONE

For over several decades now, many spiritual Masters, life coaches and certified practitioners have realized the power of spoken positive affirmations for nourishing and rejuvenating our mind, body and spirit. In the simplest terms, it is the practice of continually ingraining through thinking and of speaking positive intentions and affirmations of wellness, happiness, self esteem and abundance in very specific terms of experiencing them right here in now and being grateful for all such goodness .

Keep repeating quietly in your mind the following as you go through your day:" Health, wealth, happiness . success flows through me right now and at all times".Repeat this as often as you can during the day and just before going to sleep and upon waking up. Soon you will begin experiencing better mood, start having a positive attitude towards people and things in life and overall find good things happening all the time.

Some of the best things in the world cannot be seen or touched, as none of them are outside objects. We were born with them and they exist within us . Enjoy them through your inner senses and with your hearts. The best and most exquisite are:optimis happiness,hope, faith,peace, gratitude, love, joy, compassion and harmony. Reach within ,tap into these vast resources and start living a better life.

The saying "We become how and what we think about ourselves" not only embraces our practical experiences, but is so all inclusive as to reach out to all conditions and circumstances of our lives We literally are what we think and our characters and life patterns amount to the complete sum of all our thoughts. Our thoughts become our words over time, our words become feelings and slowly but surely our feelings manifest along positive or negative behavior patterns.

Just as plants grow from seeds, so do all our actions bloom from the in ground seeds of thought, and could not have appeared without them. This applies equally to those acts called "spontaneous" and "unplanned " as well to those which are deliberately executed.

Actions are the blossom of thought, and happiness and unhappiness are their fruits

We receive sweet or bitter fruits based on the type of seeds we plant.

"Thoughts in your minds have made you as you

are in body, mind and spirit. All what we are now started with our thoughts and finished up with their manifestations Whenever a person's mind carries evil thoughts, pain follows soon as a direct outcome

..Whenever we accept purity of thought, joy follows as surely as any law of nature We all grow through our thought process and create our own circumstances. Cause and effect is as absolute and undeviating in the hidden areas of thought as in the world of visible and material things. The human body consists of a combination of many biological systems made up with nearly 100 trillion cells. All humans are unique to the extent that there never was anybody exactly same nor will ever be the same as each of us and the combination of products, some good, some medium and some bad. They also manufacture the tools with which they build for themselves heavenly palaces of joy and strength and grace. By the right choice and true application of thought, people ascends to divine perfection; by the abuse and wrong application of thought, they descend below the level of beasts. Between these two extremes are all the grades of character, since people are their makers and masters. This may come as a profound revelation to some that we all have within ourselves the raw materials and tools to reshape ourselves in flesh and blood as the person we want to be and have within ourselves the mechanisms to live the lives of our dreams.

It is spiritually uplifting to realize our divine powers and prowess, of our oneness with the Universe with the fact hat humans are masters of their destinies, that we mold our characters, and we make and shape their conditions, environment, and lives.

.through the laws of thought;Such discoveries are totally a matter of application, self analysis, and experience.

Just as by much searching and mining, gold and diamonds are found, we all can find every truth connected with our being when we dig deep into the mine of our souls and find that we make our characters and create our lives and thus build our destinies . We will improve by watching, controlling , and altering our thoughts, tracing their effects upon ourselves, those around us and upon our life and circumstances, linking cause and effect by patient practice and investigation, and utilizing nature's every experience, even to the most trivial, everyday occurrence as a means of obtaining that knowledge of himself which is understanding,wisdom power. In this direction, as in no other, is the law is absolute .

People who seek, always find and those who try

hard succeed;sincere efforts are rewarded because with focus, dedication and consistent deeds dreams and desires are manifested.

CHAPTER TWO

For centuries engineers and scientists have focused only on finding out what can be observed and calculated. The idea that thoughts have power was not scientifically acceptable. However the facts are that thoughts do move sub-atomic particles around in our brains and our nervous systems. So, even though each neuron in the brain till now,cannot be seen and followed , the flow of neurons is tracked on MRI(magnetic resonance imaging) equipment. Such a measurable flow of neurons has a well-defined and predictable pattern of activity and they light up or "fire-up" in response to internal bodily functions or external stimuli which in turn effects precisely measurable blood flow and blood oxygen levels . The sophistication in scientific neurological measurements keeps evolving and improving, studies now reveal changes in the behavior of the chemicals that bind neurons.

There is a basis for stating that neurotransmitter cells in your brain are listening to your thoughts and picking up on the feelings within you which your thoughts produce, which leads to the conclusion that thoughts do change your body functions and life outcomes. Come to think of the grandiose centuries' old wisdom of Archimedes , who said" Give me a long and strong lever, a fulcrum and a place to stand and I will move the earth". That was not only the law of physics but also the law of positive thinking. His talking about moving the earth at that time ? How much more can your brain with scientific advancements imagine at present ? Re-arranging distant galaxies ?

Have you ever wondered why we feel defenseless at times when we read or listen to news about some dictators dominating their citizens? However there exists an easily accessible defense that goes beyond government weaponry and requires only effort to use. Within us is the power of our human mind. A recent research study focuses on the power of attraction to create wealth. Contrary to what many think, wealth accumulation isn't our most important goal .Using monetary and other resources for peace, improving the standard of living across borders and controlling global warming are more important issues when the entire world's future is at stake.

 The human mind is like a garden, which may be thoughtfully cultivated or allowed to run wild; but whether cultivated or neglected, it will grow and take shape If no useful seeds are put into it, then an abundance of useless weed-seeds will spread within and will continue to produce many weeds .However quality seeds will result in beautiful flowers and harvests.

Just as gardeners cultivate their gardens, keeping them free from weeds, and growing flowers and fruits which they plan for, so may you tend the garden of your mind, weeding out all the wrong, useless, and impure thoughts and cultivating selectively flowers and fruits of correct useful, and pure thoughts. By pursuing this process, you will sooner or later discover that you are the master-gardener of your soul, the controller of your life. Within yourself you will realize the laws of thought and accurately understand, how the thought-forces and mind patterns flow through in the shaping of your character, destiny and circumstances,character Thought and character are aligned and sincere character can only manifest itself through environment and circumstance, the outer conditions of a person's life will always be found to be coordinated with his/her inner state. This does not mean that a person's circumstances at any given time are a sign of his entire character, but that those circumstances are so intimately connected with some vital thought-elements within himself that, for the time being, they are indispensable to his development. By the law of our being, we are where and how we are living= built into our characters, thoughts have brought us there, and in the arrangement of our lives there there are no elements of chance, but everything is the result of a law which is precise and all-pervasive. This is equally true of those who feel "out of harmony" with their surroundings as are those who are satisfied with themselves.

As progressive and evolving beings, we are placed where we are so that we may learn that we can grow; and as we learn the spiritual lessons that apply to our circumstance has for us,experiences evolve giving way to newer experiences.

At any time, if you feel buffeted by circumstances it will be long as you believe yourself to be creatures of outside conditions, shake yourself up to realize that you are your creative powers, and that you can command the hidden soil and seeds of your being out of which circumstances grow, you then become their rightful masters.

Since circumstances grow out of thought every man knows who has for any length of time practiced self-control and self-purification, for he will have noticed that the alteration in his circumstances has been in exact ratio with his altered mental condition. So true is this that when a man earnestly applies himself to remedy the defects in his character, and makes swift and marked progress, he passes rapidly through a succession of marked life changes.

The soul attracts that which it secretly harbors;

that which it loves, and that which it fears; it reaches the height of its cherished aspirations; it falls to the level of its chastened desires,--and circumstances are the means by which the soul receives its own.

Every thought-seed sown or allowed to fall into the mind, and to take root there, produces its own, blossoming sooner or later into act, and bearing its own harvest of opportunity and circumstance. Good thoughts bear good fruit, bad thoughts bad fruit.

The outer world of circumstance shapes itself to the inner world of thought, and both pleasant and unpleasant external conditions are factors, which make for the ultimate good of the individual. As the reaper of his own harvest, man learns both by suffering and bliss.

Following the inmost desires, aspirations, thoughts, by which he allows himself to be dominated, (pursuing threads of impure imagination or steadfastly walking the highway of strong and high endeavor), a man at last arrives at their fulfillment in the outer conditions of his life. The laws of growth and adjustment everywhere obtains.

Circumstances do not make a person   they reveal people to their own attitudes. No such conditions can   apart from vicious inclinations, or ascending into virtue and its pure happiness without the continued cultivation of virtuous aspirations; and man, therefore, as the lord and master of thought, is the maker of himself and author of environment. Even at birth the soul comes to its own and through every step of its earthly pilgrimage it attracts those combinations of conditions which reveal itself, which are the reflections of its own purity

 People do not attract that which they want, but people draw to themselves whatever innermost thoughts they hold in their conscious and subconscious mind.. Hold thoughts of happiness, love and joy in your heart so that they get ingrained in your subconscious   and you will draw experiences which are reflected by these virtues   thoughts and desires are fed with their own food, be it foul or clean. The "divinity that shapes our ends" is in ourselves; it is our very self. In short , you can shackle yourself or set yourself free : thought and action are the jailers of Fate-- they imprison, being base; they are also the angels of Freedom--they liberate, being noble. Not what he wishes and prays for does a man get, but what he justly earns. His wishes and prayers are only gratified and answered when they harmonize with his thoughts and actions.

In the light of this truth, what, then, is the meaning of "fighting against circumstances?" It means that a man is continually revolting against an effect without, while all the time he is nourishing and preserving its cause in his heart. That cause may take the form of a conscious vice or an unconscious weakness; but whatever it is, it stubbornly retards the efforts of its possessor, and thus calls aloud for remedy.

People are anxious to improve their circumstances, but are unwilling to improve themselves; they therefore remain bound. Those who do not shrink from relentless effort can never fail to accomplish the whose sole object is to acquire wealth must be prepared to make great personal sacrifices before he can accomplish his object; and how much more so he/she who would realize a strong and well-poised life?

 basis of true prosperity, and is not only totally unfitted to rise out of his wretchedness, but is actually attracting to himself a still deeper wretchedness by dwelling in, and acting out, indolent, deceptive, and unmanly thoughts.

.

 There are several standards that humans can be compared to in terms of how much responsibility is taken up by the person the truth that man is the causer (though nearly always is unconsciously) of his circumstances, and that, whilst aiming at a good end, he is continually frustrating its accomplishment by encouraging thoughts and desires which cannot possibly harmonize with that end. Such cases could be multiplied and varied almost indefinitely, but this is not necessary, as the reader can, if he so resolves, trace the action of the laws of thought in his own mind and life, and until this is done, mere external facts cannot serve as a ground of reasoning.

Circumstances, however, are so complicated, thought is so deeply rooted, and the conditions of happiness vary so, vastly with individuals, that a man's entire soul-condition (although it may be known to himself) cannot be judged by another from the external aspect of his life alone. A man may be honest in certain directions, yet suffer privations; a man may be dishonest in certain directions, yet acquire wealth; but the conclusion usually formed that the one man fails because of his particular honesty, and that the other prospers because of his particular dishonesty, is the result of a superficial judgment, which assumes that the dishonest man is almost totally corrupt, and the honest man almost entirely virtuous. In the light of a deeper knowledge and wider experience such judgment is found to be erroneous. The dishonest man may have some admirable virtues, which the other does, not possess; and the honest man obnoxious vices which are absent in the other. The honest man reaps the good results of his honest thoughts and acts; he also brings upon himself the sufferings, which his vices produce. The dishonest man likewise garners his own suffering and happiness.

It is pleasing to human vanity to believe that one suffers because of one's virtue; but not until a man has extirpated every sickly, bitter, and impure thought from his mind, and washed every sinful stain from his soul, can he be in a place to know and declare that his sufferings are the result of his good, and not of his bad qualities; and on the way to, yet long before he has reached, that supreme perfection, he will have found, working in his mind and life, the Great Law which is absolutely just, and which cannot, therefore, give good for evil, evil for good. Possessed of such knowledge, he will then know, looking back upon his past ignorance and blindness, that his life is, and always was, justly ordered, and that all his past experiences, good and bad, were the equitable outworking of his evolving, yet unevolved self.

Good thoughts and actions can never produce bad results; bad thoughts and actions can never produce good results. This is but saying that nothing can come from corn but corn, nothing from nettles but nettles. Men understand this law in the natural world, and work with it; but few understand it in the mental and moral world (though its operation there is just as simple and undeviating), and they, therefore, do not co-operate with it.

Suffering is always the effect of wrong thought in some direction. It is an indication that the individual is out of harmony with himself, with the Law of his being. The sole and supreme use of suffering is to purify, to burn out all that is useless and impure. Suffering ceases for him who is pure. There could be no object in burning gold after the dross had been removed, and a perfectly pure and enlightened being could not suffer.

The circumstances, which a man encounters with suffering, are the result of his own mental in harmony. The circumstances, which a person encounters with blessedness, are the result of his own mental harmony. Blessedness, not material possessions, is the measure of right thought; wretchedness, not lack of material possessions, is the measure of wrong thought. A man may be cursed and rich; he may be blessed and poor. Blessedness and riches are only joined together when the riches are rightly and wisely used; and the poor man only descends into wretchedness when he regards his lot as a burden unjustly imposed.

 mental disorder. A man is not rightly conditioned until he is a happy, healthy, and prosperous being; and happiness, health, and prosperity are the result of a harmonious adjustment of the inner with the outer, of the man with his surroundings.

A person only begins to have when he ceases to

37

whine and complain , and commences to search for the hidden justice which regulates his life. And as he adapts his mind to that regulating reason, he ceases to accuse others as the cause of his condition, and builds himself up in strong and noble thoughts; ceases to kick against circumstances, but begins to use them as aids to his more rapid progress, and as a means of discovering the hidden powers and possibilities within himself.

Law, not confusion, is the dominating principle in the universe; justice, not injustice, is the soul and substance of life; and righteousness, not corruption, is the molding and moving force in the spiritual government of the world. This being so, man has but correct himself to find that the universe is right; and during the process of putting himself right he will find that as he alters his thoughts towards things and other people, things and other people will alter towards him.

The proof of this truth is in every person, and it therefore admits of easy investigation by systematic introspection and self-analysis. Let a man radically alter his thoughts, and he will be astonished at the rapid transformation it will effect in the material conditions of his life. Men imagine that thought can be kept secret, but it circumstances of destitution and disease: impure thoughts of every kind crystallize into enervating and confusing habits, which solidify into distracting and adverse circumstances: thoughts of fear, doubt, and indecision crystallize into weak, unmanly, and irresolute habits, which solidify into circumstances of failure, indigence, and slavish dependence: lazy thoughts crystallize into habits of uncleanliness and dishonesty, which solidify into circumstances of foulness and beggary: hateful and condemnatory thoughts crystallize into habits of accusation and violence, which solidify into circumstances of injury and persecution: selfish thoughts of all kinds crystallize into habits of self-seeking, which solidify into circumstances more or less distressing. On the other hand, beautiful thoughts of all kinds crystallize into habits of grace and kindliness, which solidify into genial and sunny circumstances: pure thoughts crystallize into habits of temperance and self-control, which solidify into circumstances of repose and peace: thoughts of courage, self-reliance, and decision crystallize into manly habits, which solidify into circumstances of success, plenty, and freedom: energetic thoughts crystallize into habits of cleanliness and industry, which solidify into circumstances of pleasantness: gentle and forgiving thoughts crystallize into habits of gentleness, which solidify into protective and preservative circumstances: loving and unselfish thoughts crystallize into habits of self-forgetfulness for others, which solidify into circumstances of sure and abiding prosperity and true riches.

A particular train of thought persisted in, be it good or bad, cannot fail to produce its results on the character and circumstances. A man cannot directly choose his circumstances, but he can choose his thoughts, and so indirectly, yet surely, shape his circumstances.

Nature helps every man to the gratification of the thoughts, which he most encourages, and opportunities are presented which will most speedily bring to the surface both the good and evil thoughts.

Let a man cease from his sinful thoughts, and all the world will soften towards him, and be ready to help him; let him put away his weakly and sickly thoughts, and lo, opportunities will spring up on every hand to aid his strong resolves; let him encourage good thoughts, and no hard fate shall bind him down to wretchedness and shame. The world is your kaleidoscope, and the varying combinations of colors, which at every succeeding moment it presents to you are the exquisitely adjusted pictures of your ever-moving thoughts.

"So You will be what you will to be; Let failure find its false content In that poor word, 'environment,' But spirit scorns it, and is free.

"It masters time, it conquers space; It cows Chance

that boastful trickster, and bids adieu to the tyrant Circumstance , and welcomes back the human will and determination to succeed.

"The human Will, that force unseen, The offspring of a deathless Soul, Can hew a way to any goal, Though walls of granite intervene.

"Be not impatient in delays But wait as one who understands; When spirit rises and commands The gods are ready to obey."

CHAPTER THREE

Tom rarely gets sick. And when he does, you can hardly tell. That's because he doesn't complain;he reaffirmsshe'll be in fine shape "after agood night's sleep."
Bob, however, is different as he assumes that every sniffle is a sign of a terrible disease with a dark outcome.

Needless to say,Bob gets sick more often than Tom and suffers much more than he does. One reason for their differences may perhaps be their immune systems. But an equally important factor, research studies conclude, are their attitudes..one optimistic and the other pessimistic.

According to an authentic report recently published in the Australian Health Institute Journal.

It has been confirmed that you can speed up healing by imagining the affected parts getting better. The better you are at visualizing, the stronger the effect. So the next time you come down with a cold or flu, imagine your lungs and sinuses clearing. Imagine the inflammation . reducing. Imagine yourself feeling better. It can, in all probability, get you better (Such is the power of auto-suggestion)

The theory of"mind over matter" has been proven again 1990 onward s at several research centers One set of studies used placebo pills given to diabetic patients and patients with depression who got better with the expectation of getting better as if medications were taking effect as prescribed he mind leads on the road for the body to follow and so the latter obeys directions from the mind, whether they are subconsciously expressed or explicitly stated. When thoughts are restrictive unkind and negative, one's health suffers with ailments and disease On receiving commands full of optimistic and joyful thoughts our bodies glow with beauty and youthfulness.

Health and disease, like circumstances, are rooted in thought. Sickly thoughts will express themselves through a sickly body. Thoughts of fear have been known to kill a man as surely as a weapon and they are continually killing thousands of people all the time some perhaps slowly. The people who live in fear of disease are the people who get it. Anxiety quickly demoralizes the whole body, and lays it open to the, entrance of disease;. Similarly impure thoughts, constantly held, over time shatter the nervous system.

Strong, pure, and happy thoughts build up the body with vigor,charm and grace. The body is a delicate and flexible instrument, which responds readily to the thoughts to which it is exposed to and patterns of thought produce their own effects, good or bad, whichever way.

Humans will continue to have impure and poisoned blood, so long as they encourage unclean thoughts. Out of a clean heart comes a clean life and a clean body. From a corrupt mind, an unclean body Thought is the fountain of action, life, and manifestation; make the fountain pure, and all will be pure ,radiant and healthy

Remember,merely changing your diet will not help you if you don't change your thoughts. When a person makes his thoughts pure, he/she no longer desires impure food.

Clean thoughts make clean habits. The so-called saint who does not wash his body is not a saint. He who has strengthened and purified his thoughts does not need to consider dangerous microbes.

The best way to protect your body is to guard your mind all the time. If you wish to renew your body, just beautify your mind. Thoughts of malice, envy, disappointment, desperation rob the body of its health and grace. A sour face does not come by chance; it is made by sour thoughts. Wrinkles that mark a body are created by foolishness, contempt, and mean behavior.

I have met some women in their nineties who have the bright, innocent faces of girls. I know a man well under middle age whose face is drawn into inharmonious contours. The former is the result of a sweet , positive and sunny disposition; the latter is the outcome of depression and discontent.

Just like you cannot have a sweet and wholesome unless you admit fresh air and sunshine freely into your rooms, s too a strong body and a bright, happy, or serene countenance can only result from the free admittance into the stream of thoughts of joy and goodwill and serenity.

On some faces of some the aged there are wrinkles made by sympathy, others by strong and pure thought, yet others are carved by dissatisfaction. It is easy to distinguish them,With those who have lived righteously, age is calm, peaceful, and softly mellowed, like the setting sun. I have recently seen a philosopher on his deathbed. He was not old except in years. He died as sweetly and peacefully as he had lived.

There is no physician like constant cheerful thoughts for negating the ills of the body; Good cheer and joyousness are the best remedies for dispersing the shadows of grief and sorrow. To live continually in thoughts of ill will, cynicism, suspicion, and envy, is to be confined in a self-made prison cell. But to think well of all, to be cheerful with all, to patiently learn to find the good in all--these unselfish thoughts are the very portals of heaven; and to dwell day by day in thoughts of peace towards every creature will bring abounding peace to all who possess them. Practicing meditation regularly helps people to maintain a harmonious balance between the mind, body and spirit and such harmony is an ultimate state for everybody to lead fulfilled lives

During meditation you will find your mind transcending deep within resulting in uplifting consciousness . Deep impressions, thoughts are released resulting in revitalization. Over time by repeating the process again and again ,one can feel energized, refreshed, renewed and empowered.

CHAPTER FOUR

Till such time, your thoughts are directly linked with purpose there are no meaningful accomplishments. Many people allow their thoughts to "drift without direction. Having no clear direction or goal just leads to people following a maze of unclear paths without any clarity of destination and purpose.

It's best to have clear long term vision or some purpose for your life in your mind and begin to work to achieve it. So make goals the main and focus of your thoughts. They could be inspirational or spiritual ideals or they may be material objects, nonindependent nature at certain phases of your life.; but whatever you hope and strive for aim to steadily focus your thought-forces upon goals which you have set before yourself. In fact all of us should make our goals our priority for living, and take actions to achieve them ignoring distractions and random events to put us off .

Even with a sense of focus and a clear path

towards success, outside factors can derail the most carefully laid plans. You must therefore remain driven and mentally strong while looking to achieve your goals, as you adopt a pragmatic outlook and prepare for any eventuality that may ultimately reward your ambitions.

Whether it be routine, smaller goals or a magnificent lifetime ambition, visualize yourself achieving them and receiving praise from others for being a winner. Visualization and positive affirmations will help you generate the winner mindset and supply all the energy you need. Keep focused, give it all you have and persist till you achieve your goals.

The weakest soul, knowing its own weakness, and believing this truth that strength can only be developed by effort and practice, will, thus believing, at once begin to exert itself, and, adding effort to effort, patience to patience, and strength to strength, will never stop to develop, and will at last grow divinely strong. Believe in the reality of your dreams and they will be reality one day.

One of the best skills we can acquire is to find work which excites us , makes our hearts sing and enjoy the experience of doing it to the best of our abilities. Love what you do and you will find work fulfilling.

The will to do springs from knowing that we can do it." We can do it, yes we can" slogan worked wonders for Mr Obama and got him to being the President.

 The purpose of life is finding something to live for and not merely staying alive. We have all taken birth to live out our greatest purpose and achieve our highest self. It's never too late;reorganize, reequip and reinvigorate yourself to think about how to and do whatever you can for the greatest good.

CHAPTER FIVE

Thoughts are transmitters of our intentions which create our reality. It has been proven at multiple points of time and places that if we spend enough time looking for the meaning of life and looking through self development writings that our thoughts create our world . This is not a hypothesis because all of it can be supported scientifically as accurate. Initially we way be skeptical and may have doubts about it...How can someone become a millionaire in a short while. Or just jinking about getting your pineapple peeled certainly doesn't seem to make it peel itself, so at first though this all seems baseless and impractical.

However, hold on this topic for a while When you turn on your TV and radio, pictures and sounds seem to come out of nowhere. Doesn't that sound pretty unbelievable too? And yet you get to see all those pictures and listen to the sound and music are There's certainly no tubing or inlets connecting the radio or television onto anything else. You just turn it on, and hey, there are picture sand sounds. It certainly is a real thing yet not apparently visibly connected.

"Yeah, but it's powered by electricity and there are cathode projecting photons or lids," one may say, "There's all sorts of electrons bombarding the screen, releasing energy to create the images we see. On the other side, somebody used some electricity (or other form of energy) to power their transmitter, caused some electromagnetic waves, and your receiver on your TV/radio gets those signals and converts them." In short, in goes some energy, some waves happen, and out comes some matter really far away!

Remarkable, so then, what happens when you think about this? Your thoughts are waves too! Since we don't completely understand how our brain works, isn't it possible that part of the brain is a transmitter that runs on the energy from our body, and sends out waves of thought? After all, we don't really know how thought works either! Maybe depending on the receiver at the other end, those waves are somehow converted into matter, and if thought results in actual physical matter being created, then does that not q boil down to our thoughts creating our realities?

All that you can achieve and all that you fail to achieve is the direct result of your own thoughts. In a functioning and perfect universe, where loss of balance would have negative repercussions , individual responsibility must be absolute. Your weakness and strength, purity and impurity, are your own, and not another 's; they are brought about by yourself, and and they can only be altered by yourself His condition is also his own, and not another man's. His suffering and his happiness are evolved from within. As he thinks, so he is; as he continues to think, so he remains.

A strong person cannot help a weaker unless that weaker is willing to be helped, and even then the weak person must become strong of himself; he must, by his own efforts, develop the strength which he admires in another. None but himself All of us are self-sufficient to improve ourselves. It has been usual for men to think and to say, "Many men are slaves because one is an oppressor; let us hate the oppressor." Now, however, there is among st an increasing few a tendency to reverse this judgment, and to say, "One man is an oppressor because many are slaves; let us despise the slaves."

The truth is that oppressor and slave are co-operators in ignorance, and, while seeming to afflict each other, are in reality afflicting themselves. A perfect Knowledge perceives the action of law in the weakness of the oppressed and the misapplied power of the oppressor; a perfect Love, seeing the suffering, which both states entail, condemns neither; a perfect Compassion embraces both oppressor and oppressed.

Experts have proved through study groups that people who maintained a positive attitude in all daily activities and had an active social group of six   or more people, reported fewer bodily and mental ailments and lived around 10 years more than those who did neither.

Before a man can achieve anything, even in worldly things, he must lift his thoughts above slavish animal indulgence. He may not, in order to succeed, give up all negativity and selfishness, by any means; but a portion of it must, at least, be sacrificed. A man whose first thought is bestial indulgence could neither think clearly nor plan methodically; he could not find and develop his latent resources, and would fail in any undertaking. Not having commenced to manfully control his thoughts, he is not in a position to control affairs and to adopt serious responsibilities. He is not fit to act independently and stand alone. But he is limited only by the thoughts, which he chooses.

Intellectual achievements are the result of thought consecrated to the search for knowledge, or for the beautiful and true in life and nature. Such achievements may be sometimes connected with vanity and ambition, but they are not the outcome of those characteristics; they are the natural outgrowth of long and arduous effort, and of pure and unselfish thoughts.

Spiritual achievements are the consummation of holy aspirations. He who lives constantly in the conception of noble and lofty thoughts, who dwells upon all that is pure and unselfish, will, as surely as the sun reaches its zenith and the moon its full, become wise and noble in character, and rise into a position of influence and blessedness.

Achievement, of whatever kind, is the crown of effort, the diadem of thought. By the aid of self-control, resolution, purity, righteousness, and well-directed thought a man ascends; by the aid of negativity, indolence, impurity, corruption, and confusion of thought a man descends.

A man may rise to high success in the world, and even to lofty altitudes in the spiritual realm, and again descend into weakness and wretchedness by allowing arrogant, selfish, and corrupt thoughts to take possession of him.

Victories attained by right thought can only be maintained by watchfulness. Many give way when success is assured, and rapidly fall back into failure.

All achievements, whether in the business, intellectual, or spiritual world, are the result of definitely directed thought, are governed by the same law and are of the same method; the only difference lies in the object of attainment.

People who choose to put in minimal effort may expect corresponding lower benefits. Those who consistently practice self empowerment with optimism will experience increases in happiness , health , success ans all goodness they wished for.

CHAPTER SIX

Achievements can be broken down in several steps. What may seem spectacular and seemingly impossible becomes relatively simple if you use the multiple step methodology to achieve your goals : First and foremost dream about them in happy, caring and loving ways. Dream of uplifting goals which are meaningful to you and perhaps somewhat meaningful for others as well .Dreams originate from the inner realm of the mind and it is best to quiet down the external chatter and distractions, quieten your mind and you may sometimes see the grand vision for your life, the great purpose for which you were born . Follow that up with beliefs of your being able to achieve your goals and at this stage do not let your rational mind take over with how easy or how difficult your goals seem to be, so keep a free flowing, flexible. optimistic mindset. The third step is to see them materializing and believe with with all your heart that your goals are possible just like many sports persons see themselves in their minds' eye driving that perfect swing or completing their sports' routines with perfection. To think up some examples of high goal achievements,your mental vision could range from anything like receiving the noble prize in your specialty and profession, or your performing like a celebrity super rock-star in the world's largest amphitheaters or directing your philanthropist operations across the globe with your limitless resources or perhaps controlling your $ 50 billion business empire with business operations that cater to millions of people across the world. Or choose whatever your interest and passion directs you to.

The dreamers are the saviors of the world. As the visible world is sustained by the invisible, so do some people live illustrious lives through magnificent visions while others go through mundane living with restricted thinking. Humanity has highlighted its dreamers over centuries; it will not let their ambitions ideals languish and die .It lives in them, it knows them as they realize that however lofty their goals, that they are capable and will one day realize them. So visualize your goals, clearly in your mind's eye, see yourself achieving your goals, share these goals with a close group of people. The act of sharing with a very close group reinforces your commitment and how you will bring all resources to bear on your projects. The last three steps are planning , working on them meticulously and importantly enjoying your experiences along the entire process.

Creative people as poets, authors,composers, sculptors, painters, poets, prophets, sages, among others are makers of the after-world-the architects of heaven. The world is enriched beautiful because they have lived, for without them, laboring humanity would be drab, dull and uncreative.

All those who cherish lofty, beautiful visions, high ideals in their hearts, will one day realize it. Benjamin Franklin fostered the connection between lightening and electricity and thus discovered it; The Wright brothers visioned a machine that could fly and made the first aircraft to fly safely. the Buddha (the enlightened)held the vision of a spiritual world of pristine beauty and perfect peace, and he entered into the state of enlightenment.

Cherish your visions; cherish your ideals; cherish the music that stirs in your heart, the beauty that forms in your mind, the perfection that shapes your purest thoughts, for out of them will grow all magnificent conditions, truly divine environment and a world full of radiance and beauty as long as you stay true to your pure thoughts.

To desire is to obtain; to aspire is to, achieve.

The Scriptures have stated these in uplifting works :" Ask and you shall receive,for everyone who asks receives Knock and it shall be opened to thee. Seek and you shall find . Nothing will be denied to you"(Scriptures). The values of the kindness of the Spirit have been well defined. Equally defined are the rewards of being proactive in the methodology defined in the previous section of sequential steps of dreaming, believing , conceiving , planning, working and enjoying the process. An amazing series of stepping stones for not just grand and glorious but equally relevant for better living in where and how we want to spend our lives.

Such is not the Law: such a condition of things can never obtain: "ask and receive."

All great achievement was at first and for some time just dreams. The oak sleeps in the acorn; the bird waits in the egg; and in the highest vision of the soul a waking angel stirs. Dreams are the seedlings of realities.

hard pressed by poverty and labor; confined long hours in an unhealthy workshop; unschooled, and lacking all the arts of refinement. But he dreams of better things; he thinks of intelligence, of refinement, of grace and beauty. He conceives of, mentally builds up, an ideal condition of life; the vision of a wider liberty and a larger scope takes possession of him; unrest urges him to action, and he utilizes all his spare time and means, small though they are, to the development of his latent powers and resources. Very soon so altered has his mind become that the workshop can no longer hold him. It has become so out of harmony with his mentality that it falls out of his life as a garment is cast aside, and, with the growth of opportunities, which fit the scope of his expanding powers, he passes out of it forever. Years later we see this youth as a full-grown man. We find him a master of certain forces of the mind, which he wields with worldwide influence and almost unequaled power. In his hands he holds the cords of gigantic responsibilities; he speaks, and lo, lives are changed; men and women hang upon his words and remold their characters, and, unlike, he becomes the fixed and luminous center round which innumerable destinies revolve. He has realized the Vision of his youth. He has become one with his Ideal.

And you, too, youthful reader, will realize the Vision (not the idle wish) of your heart, be it base or beautiful, or a mixture of both, for you will always gravitate toward that which you, secretly, most love. Into your hands will be placed the exact results of your own thoughts; you will receive that which you earn; no more, no less. Whatever your present environment may be, you will fall, remain, or rise with your thoughts, your Vision, your Ideal. You will become as small as your controlling desire; as great as your dominant aspiration: in the beautiful words of Stanton Kirk ham Davis, "You may be keeping accounts, and presently you shall walk out of the door that for so long has seemed to you the barrier of your ideals, and shall find yourself before an audience--the pen still behind your ear, the ink stains on your fingers and then and there shall pour out the torrent of your inspiration. You may be driving sheep, and you shall wander to the city-bucolic and open-mouthed; shall wander under the intrepid guidance of the spirit into the studio of the master, and after a time he shall say, 'I have nothing more to teach you.' And now you have become the master, who did so recently dream of great things while driving sheep. You shall lay down the saw and the plane to take upon yourself the regeneration of the world."

The thoughtless, the ignorant, and the indolent, seeing only the apparent effects of things and not the things themselves, talk of luck, of fortune, o not know the darkness and the heartaches; they only see the light and joy, and call it "luck". They do not see the long and arduous journey, but only behold the pleasant goal, and call it "good fortune," do not understand the process, but only perceive the result, and call it chance.

In all human affairs there are efforts, and there are results, and the strength of the effort is the measure of the result. Chance is not. Gifts, powers, material, intellectual, and spiritual possessions are the fruits of effort; they are thoughts completed, objects accomplished, visions realized.

The Vision that you glorify in your mind, the Ideal that you enthrone in your heart--this you will build your life by, this you will become.

CHAPTER SEVEN

Calmness of mind , body and spirit is the foundation for human growth, harmony and fulfillment. Having interacted and shared information with many scientists , preachers," life-coaches, :law-of- attraction teachers" and self-improvement gurus, the fundamental principles are consistent with all experts that firstly through our conscious efforts , practices and habits,we can reactivate our higher mind and that secondly there are enough opportunities everywhere for most people to maintain their calm state of mind and therefore that the process of reaching serene mind, body, spirit harmony is reachable and truly worthwhile regardless of individual situations and circumstances. These are results of consistently and patiently practicing self-control and calm responses to all kinds of internal feelings and external stimuli. Such peacefulness is a sign of daily , calm experiences, and an advanced exposure to the thought process and total mind, body, spirit harmony. One very simple way is to pause a few times during the day, become conscious of our breathing ,then get away a few minutes each time from whatever is going on and focus on taking long,deep breaths and exhaling slowly through the mouth, thereby enjoying the rush of energy, balance and calm for those few minutes . Repeat as and when you feel necessary. In addition ,try yet another routine of getting away from daily scheduled activities to appreciate the serenity of nature, as in easy to find common place objects as flowers which you can access a grassy patch or expanse of the outdoors and then take in the beauty and perfection of nature with all your senses and welcome those feelings of happiness, rejuvenation and freshness that flow into you from keeping close to nature.

 People can find and experience serenity in other ways as meditation, walking , taking a catnap,yoga or a body workout and which ever way you choose, you will experience multiple benefits of getting into a calmer, healthier, happier state of mind. You become calm to the extent that you understand yourself as a balanced,composed human being. knowledge Mainly because such knowledge comes with the understanding of others as the outcome of guided thinking, and as you develop the correct understanding, and see more and more clearly the continuing interactions of events by the action of cause and effect you give up anxiety, stress and negativity and instead remain poised, calm and balanced That's the state of perfect harmony between the body, mind and spirit- keep that focus on calmness and you will stay in that ideal state of harmony and natural bliss continuously.

The calm person, having learned how to govern himself/herself, knows how to adapt to others; and they, in turn, reverence his spiritual strength, and feel that they can rely on and respect such people The more relaxed a person becomes, the greater is his success, his influence, his power for good. Even the ordinary trader will find his business prosperity increase as he develops a greater self-control and equanimity, for people will always prefer to deal with a man whose demeanor is strongly equable.

The strong, calm people are always loved and revered. They are like shade-giving trees on dry terrains or sheltering rocks in the storm. "Who does not love a tranquil heart, a sweet-tempered, balanced life? It does not matter whether it rains or shines, or what changes come to those possessing these blessings, for they are always sweet, serene, and calm. That exquisite poise of character, which we call calmness is the ultimate lesson of culture, of the character of the soul. It has very high value as wisdom, more to be desired than diamonds, imagine more than even fine diamonds. How worthless does mere money accumulation look in comparison with a blissful , calm lifestyle --a life that dwells in the ocean of peace, beneath the waves, beyond the reach of hurricanes, in the vast, fathomless calm!

"How many people we know who spoil their lives, who destroy all that is precious and exquisite by violent attitudes who negate their poise of character, and make bad blood! It is a question whether the great majority of people do not destroy their lives and spoil their happiness by lack of self-control. It;s always delightful to meet people who are poised, harmonious, who have that exquisite radiance which is reflection of well -rounded personality!

If you want to make changes in your life, you must look to the causes, and the causes are almost always the way you are using your mind — the way you are thinking. You cannot think both negative and positive thoughts at the same time. One or the other will dominate. The mind is a slave of habit, so it becomes each individual's responsibility to make sure that positive emotions and thoughts join the dominating influence in their mind.

In order to change external conditions, you must first change the internal. Most people omit this step. They try to change external conditions by working directly on those conditions. This always proves futile, or at best temporary, unless it is accompanied by a change of thoughts and beliefs.

Awakening to this truth, the way to a better, more successful life becomes crystal clear. Train your conscious mind to think thoughts of success, happiness, health, prosperity, and to weed out negativity such as fear and worry. Keep your conscious mind busy with the expectation of the best, and make sure the thoughts you habitually think are based upon what you want to see happen in your life.

Water takes the shape of whatever container holds it, whether it be in a glass, a vase or a riverbank. Likewise, your mind will create and manifest according to the images you habitually think about in your daily thinking. This is how your destiny is created. A new life is created by new thoughts.

We have much to be grateful for here at unlimited opportunity to share the love, knowledge and understanding that we have received, with you. Together we can make a positive impact on the whole world.

When we know ourselves, we know that everything in existence is love expressing intelligently through energy. We are that and so is everyone and everything else. Separateness is only in form. We see energy manifested in different forms. These forms are created by thought. We believe that we are separate because we are not aware of our wholeness.

All of this awareness and experience is available to us through the development of our right brain abilities. When we begin to work with a process for releasing stress and strengthening or refining our nervous systems, we begin to discover who we are on a deeper level and soon begin to know the wholeness that includes all of us and everything else in existence. When this happens we begin to understand that all aspects of life are governed by laws of nature or principles of life, and we start to see what these principles are, and how they work. At this point we move into a much more advanced level of functioning, and discover that we have the power right within ourselves to create whatever we choose.

CHAPTER EIGHT

Given here is a methodology for empowering yourself. These are ways for improvement from where you are to still higher ,happier states of fulfilled living Use these simple techniques to activate your mind to higher levels of consciousness:

a. Trust the Universe. First and foremost,remind yourself of and commit yourself to accepting higher energies and the greater good of the Universe. We all are truly spiritual beings living in human forms and by trusting the Universe we remind ourselves that we are safe, secure and well and the belief that the Universe will provide is reassurance that we are here to further certain lifetime goals. We have access to all resources of nature and we are complete in every way. Life is meant to be well lived and intrinsic faith, optimism and our efforts make it so.

b. Release negativity : Internalize and repeat this statement at regular intervals during the day: "I am willing to release all negative patterns in my consciousness by wrapping them with love and letting them float far,far, far away into nothingness. I keep positive and" I radiate all goodness at all times"

c. Forgive:the process of forgiveness covers letting go of the past and coming into the present. Forgiving is also making peace with our self,it is releasing all negative patterns of hurt and judgment that we have held onto. and being at peace with the world. Set yourself being calm, serene and synchronized with powerful, positive energies.

For this try the simple practice of repeating regularly : "I forgive myself and everybody for everything in all dimensions of time and space". All others also forgive me for everything in all times and space. I am released , free and in total peace. My existence is peaceful" Feel yourself relaxed , empowered and re-energized.

We all normally get involved with our individual routine activities at home , at work, with our hobbies and leisure activities that we lose sight of our primary purpose of leading fulfilled lives .This is worth correcting. Think about your priorities, set hem out clearly and focus on your intentions.

Begin with setting out affirmations for daily use

Several times daily, think about affirmations of positive intentions: My family and I are receiving abundance of health , happiness, success and all good things in life right now and for all times.

e. Correct breathing

Breathing is our life force. . Rhythmic, controlled , deep breathing literally moves life energy throughout our body vitalizing every cell and system of our being. By gaining awareness of our breath and learning to control it, we can control our physical,mental and spiritual state. Pause and sense the movement and pattern of the breath. Realize the usefulness of controlled breathing to our overall well being. When life feels stressful and we feel out of control, we can calm our breath. Slow it down and deepen it. Several times a day, take time off for few minutes for enjoyable, controlled breathing by taking in deep breaths through the nose , holding for a minute and breathing out through the mouth.

e. Recall and dwell on your achievements

Train your mind to find the positives by listing your strengths. Write down personal achievements, family achievements,those at workorin society,goals you have met, things you have done well, and places you have visited.

Too often we spend time thinking about what isn't right in our lives instead of focusing on what's right.

So switch to the positives , things that you have done well and all your good experiences till date. Remember the golden law: what you focus on expands, so bring your thoughts back to the good things in life.

It's worth repetition that you focus, focus, focus only on things you think you have done right , think of all positives about who you are and all that you have. Just keep going with only all what is right and you will be amazed by the large number of correct the rights you can think of.

f. Live in the present. Having dwelt on all correct things of the past, realize you are here and everything is what is happening this present moment. More importantly our tomorrows are created by our thoughts now , right here and now- the So it is key focus on our present moment, be grateful for all the abundance we have and that we are loved , lovable and loving because we exist. It's a glorious moment and our future is radiantly fulfilled

The best time to work towards what we want is when thoughts are fresh in our minds and the motivation is strong for us to move forward . Live in the now. , so do it today. Do it now." By affirming right here and now that all is well and in perfect order, you are creating that very sense of perfection of what you are affirming to enjoy better, fulfilled living. Repeating positive affirmations in the quietness of your mind or aloud is a really powerful recipe for mind, body, spirit fulfillment.

In fact a short,. successful "call"for reality manifestation involves (at least) two elements:

1. A clear statement of belief or intent, spoken or heldin a positive way........followed immediately by a

2. complete release of the outcome into the hands of the Source.

A person doesn't manifest his or her world out of nothing either,each of you forms your personal reality from the *everything,* which exists all around you. In order to make something physical, you simply focus upon it.....(which slows down the vibration sufficiently for it to solidify), and then you install perceptual veils around it, to block Mouthe awareness of everything else that is there. This is your own perceptual equivalent of putting blinders on a horse.

As you begin your process of focusing, you must clearly realize how the creative element of your mind works. T he explanation we are going to make for you now is a linear one,because you are now operating within a linear reality base. Please realize that you have the power to change the order or the rules of this process at any time.

Your affirmative statements, especially when accompanied by true desire and passion, are like God granting you everything you could ever wish for. As has been experienced, tested and researched: your beliefs become reality and there is no differentiation between what is real and what was a vision some time ago." Divinity does this through your own declarations of what is, not through declarations of *what is not.

Therefore, when a person declares, within himself: I don't want to smoke" am not going to be angry today," e creative manifesting Mind hears (and responds to) an affirmative version of those statements. What it hears is: "I do want to smoke," and "I am going to feel depressed today."

You must realize that physical reality is created from focus. f you are constantly focusing upon what you *don't want," and not on what you *do want, your manifestation power will tend cot follow that focus. The center of power in a Call to manifest is located between the subject and the desired (or declared) action or outcome. he commands are stacked and prioritized in your printer, according to e following factors:

The "level" of self that is making the command (The snore expanded aspects of you get the most clout when it comes to ordering up your manifestations)

2.The desire, intensity, and clarity behind the declaration.

3.Stating your intentions clearly, by thought, in writing and verbally and making the stated intentions become reality.

Clearly making a statement of want and intent leaves an energy field impression in the "reality bubble" of a person's existence. It registers, whether the person is aware of it or not. command gets introduced. If the stated intention is not reversed by an opposite intention   , the creative goal- seeking mechanism will continue to put together options, alternatives and the sequence for bringing the goals into reality.

To create an intention , and then to worry it, creates an attitude of doubt in your creative ability. It's like starting to enjoy good food with 10 critical people showing disapproval.Sure enough, fairly quickly you may get indigestion or an upset stomach.

 Believe and expect the best and the Universe will materialize your goals,dreams and desires(from the Scriptures)

Optimism, Hope and Faith can manifest miracles(translated from the Vedas)

From as early as the Scriptures and the Vedas to the recent research at top worldwide institutions , findings and writings confirm the universal truth remains ever constant " Your thoughts shape your world and that optimism is most important for happiness. Besides, optimism is the best skill and

habit of all successful people. Thought power is the key for creating your reality. Your thoughts entirely create your lives and your experiences.- not just partially but precisely and completely. Your life is what you make of it with your thoughts.

Everything you perceive in the physical world has its origin in the invisible, inner world of your thoughts and beliefs. To become the master of your destiny, you must learn to control the nature of your dominant, habitual thoughts. By doing so, you will be able to attract into your life all what you intend to have and to experience . The power of positive thinking can help you to achieve anything once you come to accept the truth that your thoughts create your reality.- right now and for all times. You are entirely the creators of your own realities,every time and under all circumstances You yourselves shape your lives with your thoughts, feelings and beliefs. At first glance the above may seem irrelevant, baseless or implausible because you may instantly point to events that seem to be beyond your control:your birth circumstances, some illnesses, some accidents, your oppressors, and that earthquake or storm that killed so many. And of course if you were to count only our present or recent conscious thoughts, then the first truth may initially seem irrational. No one says to themselves, "I think it's time I got harmed, mugged or cheated."

So let me define this universal truth more accurately. At mostly subconscious levels— starting before birth and then fueled by the accumulated paradigm of thoughts, feelings and beliefs that were once subconscious —you created them all: every event, detail and nuance of your lives.

 Become aware that you are a part of the great consciousness. You are a fragment of the Universe and you forget your wholeness that your mental adventures can be real. The day you live this truth and take conscious control of your thoughts is the day you declare your freedom and begin your mastery of life.

 The truth above compliments the laws of contemporary science and metaphysics .Modern scientists, hunting for the fundamental building blocks of the universe are discovering other laws. Here's one: both the existence and the behavior of subatomic particles depend on what is going on in the mind of the scientist". Yes, you read that correctly. It's not a misprint and it's not fringe science; it has been replicated many times. The implications are stunning. As one science researcher put it, "Physicists these days are discovering untapped frontiers."

Traditional science assumes that consciousness arises from physical objects. Metaphysics states that the reverse is true too, which Asian Hindu teachers have known for more than 3,000 years. And the Buddha put it this way: "All that we are is the result of what we have thought. The mind is everything. What we think is what we are and we become."

"Imagine a herd of horses, grazing in a field, a few in the sunlight, but most in the shadows of the nearby forest. Let the herd represent your accumulated thoughts, feelings and, above all, your beliefs, which have more power over your life than a hurricane. You raised every horse, feeding them thoughts in the stable of your mind, never knowing what powerful creatures they would become after they slipped quietly into the shadows. And the most powerful of all are completely hidden in the depths—your invisible beliefs."

You might ask, how can a belief be invisible? Surely if it's a belief, must you not be aware of it?

But that's only true of your weakest beliefs. If you think that,then, yes, you're aware of a low-power belief. If you believe that then you?re aware of a belief with more power to direct your choices. However, if you know that, you see it as the truth and fail to recognize a potent belief that shapes your life. If you know that eating animals incurs karmic debt, you avoid the butcher. If you know that teenagers are trouble, you create parenting problems. If you know you will lose your faculties as you age, it is the knowing, not the age, that damages you.

And the most powerful of all your beliefs is the simplest: the assumption-belief. That's a certainty so deep it seems nonsense to question it. Countless millions are bound by assumption-beliefs that make their lives a misery. And yet all beliefs began with the accumulation of your thoughts. Many of those thoughts began before your birth, creating the highway of your life. The rest—those that determine which lanes you travel in that highway —are thoughts that you hold or once held in this lifetime.

Yes, even your physical health is caused by your accumulation of subconscious beliefs. Which can be terribly difficult to accept—because it suggests that if you catch, say, leukemia, it's your fault! But the word is not fault, it is cause. No blame or judgment is appropriate because your most potent beliefs grow in your shadows and your mind usually has no idea of its own potent powers.

You might ask what specific thought, feeling or belief could cause a specific illness.?That;s like asking if a rain shower from a dark, overcast sky came from one cloud. Instead its logical to assume that persistent thoughts l of being powerless and of being a victim compounded by suppressed emotions like anger, hatred, and fear will inevitably express themselves in your body. To sum up, the illness or that setback too was your creation.

You become what you think of most what you feel follows you, what you believe builds around you.

If perhaps you are wondering: if we get what we focus on, why do we get so much of what we don't want? That is because we often focus most passionately on what we don't want, and our personal universe always grants our greatest passions. That is so important to understand. Always ?yes?. So if you wish for a million dollars but despair at your poverty, which of those two passions will manifest?Here is the most painfully destructive level of creation-belief. That you're not the creator of your life, but a victim of circumstance.? You blame your condition on something other than yourself: God, the stars, fate, birth, parents, lovers, the government, accidents, sickness, the police. You never stood a chance. You are inherently worthless. You are a victim and life is a torment. Is that you?

If not, try the next level, more evolved: you are sometimes the creator of your life. You can influence some events, but mostly, external forces are too strong to fight. You blame most of your condition on something other than yourself. You take some responsibility for what happens to you. You have some worth, some potential. Life is a struggle with a few highlights. Is that you?

Here's the next level: you are mostly the creator of your life. You can influence most events, though sometimes external forces are too great. You take responsibility for most of your actions. You spend little time blaming others for painful events. You are a worthwhile person with faults. You have a lot of potential. Life is an interesting and often enjoyable challenge. Is that you?

If not, then try this one. The master level of creation- the belief is that you are entirely the creator of your life. You are part of the great field of consciousness that- being which has many adventures and many faces, including yours. You do not see your earth character as you, but as your work of art. Your every thought, attitude and action is your choice. You are fully responsible, not only for your creations but for your response to your creations. You never blame or judge others for your experiences. Your inherent worth and potential are vast. Life is an exciting, sometimes surprising, sometimes painful, yet joyous adventure.

Is that you?Do you see the great pattern here? Whatever level of creation-belief you hold you will create the conditions that appear to prove you right. What you believe will be manifest around you.

That is the viability of the first universal truth. Believe and embrace happiness, health,love , peace , harmony , joy, fulfillment , self-love and self worth and experience all these in abundance every moment of your life. I was once told by my mother, which many children get to hear:not to behave as if the entire, vast universe revolved around me". In fact, it does. Or rather, my universe does. And so does yours. Literally. As quantum physics is beginning to discover, there are an infinite number of universes. Your consciousness s revolve around you, creating all that you know and experience and the trillion plus cells in your body and mind. You are the butterfly in a bubble of your making. Your bubble overlaps with the bubbles of others. Every direction you head in ie your body, mind and spirit, you create and every event and detail of your experiences.

The ten most beautiful things in the world cannot be seen or touched, as none of them are external things. We were born with them and they exist within us. Feel them through your inner senses and with your hearts. The Best and the most Beautiful are:Optimism, Happiness, Hope, Peace,Faith,Gratitude, Love,Compassion, ,Peace and Harmony.... Reach within ,tap into your vast resources and empower your lives.

of any mere external force; the criminal thought had long been secretly fostered in the heart, and the hour of opportunity revealed its gathered power. Circumstances do not make the man; they reveal him to himself No such conditions can exist as descending into vice and its attendant sufferings apart from vicious inclinations, or ascending into virtue and its pure happiness without the continued cultivation of virtuous aspirations; and man, therefore, as the lord and master of thought, is the maker of himself and author of environment. Even at birth the soul comes to its own and through every step of its earthly pilgrimage it attracts those combinations of conditions which reveal itself, which are the reflections of its own purity and, impurity, its strength and weakness.

 people do not attract that which they want, but that which they are. Their whims, fancies, and ambitions are thwarted at every step, but their inmost thoughts and desires are fed with their own food, be it foul or clean. The "divinity that shapes our ends" is in ourselves; it is our very self. In short , you can shackle yourself or set yourself free : thought and action are the jailers of Fate--they imprison, being base; they are also the angels of Freedom--they liberate, being noble. Not what he wishes and prays for does a man get, but what he justly earns. His wishes and prayers are only gratified and answered when they harmonize with his thoughts and actions.

In the light of this truth, what, then, is the meaning of "fighting against circumstances?" It means that a man is continually revolting against an effect without, while all the time he is nourishing and preserving its cause in his heart. That cause may take the form of a conscious vice or an unconscious weakness; but whatever it is, it stubbornly retards the efforts of its possessor, and thus calls aloud for remedy.

People, in general, are willing to improve their lives, yet not willing to change themselves for the better; they therefore stay stuck in their grooves and in their things as they are.. Those who are open to putting in efforts are normally rewarded by getting what they had wished for. Goals could vary from average standards of health, wealth and happiness to the highest and loftiest desires. Whether people primarily choose wealth accumulation or a combination of billionaire status along with worldwide political status and global recognition, there is smart thinking and a lot of effort to be put in along the way.

ch a man does not understand the simplest rudiments of those principles which are the basis of true prosperity, and is not only totally unfitted to rise out of his wretchedness, but is actually attracting to himself a still deeper wretchedness by dwelling in, and acting out, indolent, deceptive, and unmanly thoughts.

Here is a rich man who is the victim of a painful and persistent disease as the result of gluttony. He is willing to give large sums of money to get rid of it, but he will not sacrifice his gluttonous desires. He wants to gratify his taste for rich and unnatural viands and have his health as well. Such a man is totally unfit to have health, because he has not yet learned the first principles

I have introduced these three cases merely as illustrative of the truth that man is the causer (though nearly always is unconsciously) of his circumstances, and that, whilst aiming at a good end, he is continually frustrating its accomplishment by encouraging thoughts and desires which cannot possibly harmonize with that end. Such cases could be multiplied and varied almost indefinitely, but this is not necessary, as the reader can, if he so resolves, trace the action of the laws of thought in his own mind and life, and until this is done, mere external facts cannot serve as a ground of reasoning.

Circumstances, however, are so complicated, thought is so deeply rooted, and the conditions of happiness vary so, vastly with individuals, that a man's entire soul-condition (although it may be known to himself) cannot be judged by another from the external aspect of his life alone. A man may be honest in certain directions, yet suffer privations; a man may be dishonest in certain directions, yet acquire wealth; but the conclusion usually formed that the one man fails because of his particular honesty, and that the other prospers because of his particular dishonesty, is the result of a superficial judgment, which assumes that the dishonest man is almost totally corrupt, and the honest man almost entirely virtuous. In the light of a deeper knowledge and wider experience such judgment is found to be erroneous. The dishonest man may have some admirable virtues, which the other does, not possess; and the honest man obnoxious vices which are absent in the other. The honest man reaps the good results of his honest thoughts and acts; he also brings upon himself the sufferings, which his vices produce. The dishonest man likewise garners his own suffering and happiness.

It is pleasing to human vanity to believe that one suffers because of one's virtue; but not until a man has extirpated every sickly, bitter, and impure thought from his mind, and washed every sinful stain from his soul, can he be in a place to know and declare that his sufferings are the result of his good, and not of his bad qualities; and on the way to, yet long before he has reached, that supreme perfection, he will have found, working in his mind and life, the Great Law which is absolutely just, and which cannot, therefore, give good for evil, evil for good. Possessed of such knowledge, he will then know, looking back upon his past ignorance and blindness, that his life is, and always was, justly ordered, and that all his past experiences, good and bad, were the equitable outworking of his evolving, yet imperfect self.

Good thoughts and actions can never produce bad

results; bad thoughts and actions can never produce good results. This is but saying that nothing can come from corn but corn, nothing from nettles but nettles. Men understand this law in the natural world, and work with it; but few understand it in the mental and moral world (though its operation there is just as simple and undeviating), and they, therefore, do not co-operate with it.

Suffering is always the effect of wrong thought in some direction. It is an indication that the individual is out of harmony with himself, with the Law of his being. The sole and supreme use of suffering is to purify, to burn out all that is useless and impure. Suffering ceases for him who is pure. There could be no object in burning gold after the dross had been removed, and a perfectly pure and enlightened being could not suffer.

The circumstances, which a man encounters with suffering, are the result of his own mental in harmony. The circumstances, which a man encounters with blessedness, are the result of his own mental harmony. Blessedness, not material possessions, is the measure of right thought; wretchedness, not lack of material possessions, is the measure of wrong thought. A man may be cursed and rich; he may be blessed and poor. Blessedness and riches are only joined together when the riches are rightly and wisely used; and the poor man only descends into wretchedness when he regards his lot as a burden unjustly imposed.

Indigence and indulgence are the two extremes of wretchedness. They are both equally unnatural and the result of mental disorder. A man is not rightly conditioned until he is a happy, healthy, and prosperous being; and happiness, health, and prosperity are the result of a harmonious adjustment of the inner with the outer, of the man with his surroundings.

A man only begins to be a man when he ceases to whine and revile, and commences to search for the hidden justice which regulates his life. And as he adapts his mind to that regulating factor, he ceases to accuse others as the cause of his condition, and builds himself up in strong and noble thoughts; ceases to kick against circumstances, but begins to use them as aids to his more rapid progress, and as a means of discovering the hidden powers and possibilities within himself.

Law, not confusion, is the dominating principle in the universe; justice, not injustice, is the soul and substance of life; and righteousness, not corruption, is the molding and moving force in the spiritual government of the world. This being so, man has but to correct himself to find that the universe is right; and during the process of putting himself right he will find that as he alters his thoughts towards things and other people, things and other people will alter towards him.

The proof of this truth is in every person, and it therefore admits of easy investigation by systematic introspection and self-analysis. Let a man radically alter his thoughts, and he will be astonished at the rapid transformation it will effect in the material conditions of his life. Men imagine that thought can be kept secret, but it cannot; it rapidly crystallizes into habit, and habit solidifies into circumstance. Bestial thoughts crystallize into habits of drunkenness and sensuality, which solidify into circumstances of destitution and disease: impure thoughts of every kind crystallize into enervating and confusing habits, which solidify into distracting and adverse circumstances: thoughts of fear, doubt, and indecision crystallize into weak, unmanly, and irresolute habits, which solidify into circumstances of failure, indigence, and slavish dependence: lazy thoughts crystallize into habits of uncleanliness and dishonesty, which solidify into circumstances of foulness and beggary: hateful and condemnatory thoughts crystallize into habits of accusation and violence, which solidify into circumstances of injury and persecution: selfish thoughts of all kinds crystallize into habits of self-seeking, which solidify into circumstances more or less distressing. On the other hand, beautiful thoughts of all kinds crystallize into habits of grace and kindliness, which solidify into genial and sunny circumstances: pure thoughts crystallize into habits of temperance and self-control, which solidify into circumstances of repose and peace: thoughts of courage, self-reliance, and decision crystallize into manly habits, which solidify into circumstances of success, plenty, and freedom: energetic thoughts crystallize into habits of cleanliness and industry, which solidify into circumstances of pleasantness: gentle and forgiving thoughts crystallize into habits of gentleness, which solidify into protective and preservative circumstances: loving and unselfish thoughts crystallize into habits of self-forgetfulness for others, which solidify into circumstances of sure and abiding prosperity and true riches.

A particular train of thought persisted in, be it good or bad, cannot fail to produce its results on the character and circumstances. A man cannot directly choose his circumstances, but he can choose his thoughts, and so indirectly, yet surely, shape his circumstances.

Nature helps every man to the gratification of the thoughts, which he most encourages, and opportunities are presented which will most speedily bring to the surface both the good and evil thoughts.

Let a man cease from his sinful thoughts, and all

the world will soften towards him, and be ready to help him; let him put away his weakly and sickly thoughts, and lo, opportunities will spring up on every hand to aid his strong resolves; let him encourage good thoughts, and no hard fate shall bind him down to wretchedness and shame. The world is your kaleidoscope, and the varying combinations of colors, which at every succeeding moment it presents to you are the exquisitely adjusted pictures of your ever-moving thoughts.

"So You will be what you will to be; Let failure find its false content In that poor word, 'environment,' But spirit scorns it, and is free.

"It masters time, it conquers space; It cows Chance that boastful trickster, and bids adieu to the tyrant Circumstance , and welcomes back the human will and determination to succeed.

"The human Will, that force unseen, The offspring of a deathless Soul, Can hew a way to any goal, Though walls of granite intervene.

"Be not impatient in delays But wait as one who understands; When spirit rises and commands The gods are ready to obey."

The body is the servant of the mind. It obeys

directions from the mind, whether they be deliberately chosen or subconsciously expressed. When the thoughts are negative restrictive and unkind the body sinks rapidly into disease and imbalance. At the command of joyous and healthy thoughts it becomes clothed with youthfulness and beauty.

Disease and health, like circumstances, are rooted in thought. Sickly thoughts will express themselves through a sickly body. Thoughts of fear have been known to kill a man as surely as a weapon and they are continually killing thousands of people all the time though less rapidly. The people who live in fear of disease are the people who get it. Anxiety quickly demoralizes the whole body, and lays it open to the, entrance of disease;. Similarly impure thoughts, even if not physically indulged, over time shatter the nervous system.

Strong, pure, and happy thoughts build up the body with vigor, radiance and grace. The body is a delicate and flexible instrument, which responds readily to the thoughts to which it is exposed to and habits of thought will produce their own effects, good or bad, whichever way.

Humans will continue to have impure and poisoned blood, so long as they encourage unclean thoughts. Out of a clean heart comes a clean life and a clean body. Out of a defiled mind proceeds a defiled life and a corrupt body. Thought is the fountain of action, life, and manifestation; make the fountain pure, and all will be pure ,radiant and healthy

Merely by altering your diet will not help you if you don't improve your thoughts. When a person makes his/her thoughts purified, he/she no longer desires unhealthy. stale food.

Cleanliness is both a virtue and a state of mind .Clean thoughts make clean habits. The self-proclaimed called saint who does not wash his body is not fully clean and purified. People who have strengthened and purified their thoughts do not need to consider unhealthy microbes.

The best way to protect your body is to guard your mind all the time. Whenever you decide to cleanse and renew yourself, start with making your mind beautiful. Thoughts of revenge envy, disappointment, desperation cut the body's radiance, health and harmony. Having a sad face is not accidental; it is a direct result of negative, sad thoughts. Unhealthy wrinkles that show up on bodies are created by maintaining negative thoughts of hatred, jealousy, contempt and similar negative thought patterns.

It is not difficult to find some women in their eighties who have bright, innocent faces of youthful girls. I also know a man well under middle age whose face is drawn into a distorted, ungracious profile. The former is the result of joyful ,vibrant, positively sweet attitudes and the latter is the outcome of unhappiness, depression and discontent.

Just like by admitting lot's of fresh air and sunshine you can have bright, sweet smelling rooms, by keeping a flow of joyful, sincere, beneficial thoughts you can have a healthy, happy body and a glowing personality.

Try being analytical to differentiate people with wrinkles brought about by their strength,sympathy and concerned thinking as against some others wrinkled by worry, dissatisfaction and negative thought patterns. . them,With those who have lived righteously, age is calm, peaceful, and softly mellowed, like the setting sun. I have recently seen a philosopher on his deathbed. He was not old except in years. He died as sweetly and peacefully as he had lived.

There is no physician like constant cheerful thoughts for negating the ills of the body; Good cheer and joyousness are the best remedies for dispersing the shadows of grief and sorrow. To live continually in thoughts of ill will, cynicism, suspicion, and envy, is to be confined in a self-made prison cell. But to think well of all, to be cheerful with all, to patiently learn to find the good in all--these unselfish thoughts are the very portals of heaven; and to dwell day by day in thoughts of peace towards every creature will bring abounding peace to all who possess them. Practicing meditation regularly helps people to maintain a harmonious balance between the mind, body and spirit and such harmony is an ultimate state for everybody to lead fulfilled lives

During meditation you will find your mind transcending deep within resulting in uplifting consciousness . Deep impressions, thoughts are released resulting in revitalization. Over time by repeating the process again and again ,one can feel energized, refreshed, renewed and empowered.

Meditative states are when thoughts subside. Thoughts come up,pause and pass through. Do you recognize them in this list: Desires, ambitions, expectations, doubts, unpleasant memories,

Until thoughts are linked with purpose there are no meaningful accomplishments. Most people allow their thoughts to "drift" upon the ocean of life. Aimlessness just leads to people following a maze of foggy paths without any clarity of destination and end result.

Those who have no central purpose in their life fall an easy prey to petty worries, fears, troubles, and self pity, all of which are indications of weakness, which lead, just as surely as deliberately planned sins (though by a different route), to failure, unhappiness, and loss, since weakness cannot persist in a powerful evolving universe.

You should conceive of legitimate purposes in your heart, and set out to accomplish them. So make purposes the core and focus of your thoughts. It may take the form of a spiritual ideal, or it may be a worldly object, according to your nature at the time during that time period; but whatever you hope and wish for aim to steadily focus your thought-forces upon goals which you have set before yourself. We should make our goals our priority for living, and take action to achieve them ignoring distractions and random events thoughts to put us off course longings, and imaginings. This is the royal road to self-control and true concentration of thought. Even if he fails again and again to accomplish his purpose (as he necessarily must until weakness is overcome), the strength of character gained will be the measure of his true success, and this will form a new starting-point for future power and triumph.

Those who are not ready for the apprehension of a great purpose should fix the thoughts upon the faultless performance of their duty, no matter how insignificant their task may seem. Only in this way can the thoughts be gathered and focused, and resolution and energy be developed, which being done, there is nothing which may not be accomplished.

Our cumulative thoughts gather strength over time and when harnessed through constant effort and practice, can help us overcome all weakness and failings. Research studies through control groups have established that physical and mental well-being can be improved significantly by incorporating consistent patterns of uplifting, positive thoughts- thoughts of gratitude,self-worth, confidence, love, caring, sharing, happiness, laughter.

One of the best skills we can acquire is to find work which excites us , makes our hearts sing and enjoy the experience of doing it to the best of our abilities. Love what you do and you will find work fulfilling.

The will to do springs from the knowledge that we can do. Doubt and fear are the great enemies of knowledge, who does not slay them. thwarts

He who has conquered doubt and fear has conquered failure. His every, thought is allied with power, and all difficulties are bravely met and wisely overcome. His purposes are seasonably planted, and they bloom and bring forth fruit- in fact an abundant harvest.

Thought allied fearlessly to purpose becomes creative force: he who knows this is ready to become something higher and stronger than a mere bundle of wavering thoughts and fluctuating sensations; he who does this has become the conscious and intelligent wielder of his

All that you can achieve and all that you fail to achieve is the direct result of your own thoughts. In a fair and perfect universe, where loss of balance would have negative repercussions , individual responsibility must be absolute. A man's weakness and strength, purity and impurity, are his own, and not another man's; they are brought about by himself, and not by another; and they can only be altered by himself, never by another. His condition is also his own, and not another man's. His suffering and his happiness are evolved from within. As he thinks, so he is; as he continues to think, so he remains.

A strong person cannot help a weaker unless that weaker is willing to be helped, and even then the weak person must become strong of himself; he must, by his own efforts, develop the strength which he admires in another. None but himself All of us are self-sufficient to improve ourselves.

It has been usual for men to think and to say, "Many men are slaves because one is an oppressor; let us hate the oppressor." Now, however, there is among st an increasing few a tendency to reverse this judgment, and to say, "One man is an oppressor because many are slaves; let us despise the slaves."

The truth is that oppressor and slave are co-operators in ignorance, and, while seeming to afflict each other, are in reality afflicting themselves. A perfect Knowledge perceives the action of law in the weakness of the oppressed and the misapplied power of the oppressor; a perfect Love, seeing the suffering, which both states entail, condemns neither; a perfect Compassion embraces both oppressor and oppressed.

He who has conquered weakness, and has put away all selfish thoughts, belongs neither to oppressor nor oppressed. He is free.

A man can only rise, conquer, and achieve by lifting up his thoughts. He can only remain weak, and abject, and miserable by refusing to lift up his thoughts.

Before a man can achieve anything, even in worldly things, he must lift his thoughts above slavish animal indulgence. He may not, in order to succeed, give up all negativity and selfishness, by any means; but a portion of it must, at least, be sacrificed. A man whose first thought is bestial indulgence could neither think clearly nor plan methodically; he could not find and develop his latent resources, and would fail in any undertaking. Not having commenced to manfully control his thoughts, he is not in a position to control affairs and to adopt serious responsibilities. He is not fit to act independently and stand alone. But he is limited only by the thoughts, which he chooses.

There can be no progress, no achievement without sacrifice, and a man's worldly success will be in the measure that he sacrifices his confused animal thoughts, and fixes his mind on the development of his plans, and the strengthening of his resolution and self-reliance. And the higher he lifts his thoughts, the more manly, upright, and righteous he becomes, the greater will be his success, the more blessed and enduring will be his achievements. The laws of the Universe are straightforward: we receive what we give out on the long run. Rational, well-planned , honest efforts help everyone achieve worthwhile goals.

me Over the ages, many learned and spiritual Masters , the world over, have taught us that the path to empowerment and fulfillment is through uplifting human thought elements and through beneficial actions and that the path of noble thoughts and deeds is truly the most virtuous.

Intellectual achievements are the result of thought processes which are dedicated and concentrated on seeking out knowledge, or concepts that are benevolent and purposeful for life and for nature. Here is the universally accepted concept for better living: People who strive for and achieve unselfish , noble, beneficial thought patterns find themselves living and enjoying wonderful and joyous experiences. For letting go of negative thought patterns, its useful to practice affirming that we are willing to release all negative patterns within our subconscious in a gentle , loving way and letting negative patterns within us fly out into a far away nothingness from which they may have come from. Affirmations to accept positive thought patterns are welcome messages and methods for retaining with us only what is good and beneficial. To summarize , its the process of gently releasing all conscious and subconscious negative patterns within ourselves and inviting within positive thought patterns to stay within. This may seem naive or simplistic, but you will be surprised with the transformation that this can bring into one's life. Many other experts have talked and written about these basics of rinsing out the unwanted and bringing in the positives in our lives.

A man may rise to high success in the world, and even to lofty altitudes in the spiritual realm, and again descend into weakness and wretchedness by allowing arrogant, selfish, and corrupt thoughts to take possession of him.

All achievements, whether in the business, intellectual, or spiritual world, are the result of definitely directed thought, are governed by the same law and are of the same method; the only difference lies in the object of attainment.

It is helpful to to visualize one's goalsto achieve them.Here you will learn some visualization techniques that will help you visualize better   and manifest your desires.When done properly, visualization helps you meet almost any goal.

Almostallsuccessfulpeople, including sportspersons use visualization to achieve their goals. Some do it knowingly, others do it as a reflex action,since they haverepeatedly practiced and mastered the techniques.

First, find a quiet place – where you won't be

disturbed. We don't want a break when we are talking to our subconscious. You can visualize -

First thing in the morning, while still in bed. You can go to the bathroom, relieve yourself and come back and visualize.

When riding the bus or the subway.

Waiting your turn at the supermarket or anywhere else.

Sitting on the coach, instead of watching Television.

When waiting for someone.

Last thing at night before falling asleep.

 The dreamers are the saviors of the world. As the visible world is sustained by the invisible, so men, through all their trials and sins and sordid vocations, are nourished by the beautiful visions of their solitary dreamers. Humanity cannot forget its dreamers; it cannot let their ideals fade and die; it lives in them; it knows them as they realities which it shall one day see and know.

 People who pursue their enhanced dreams and visions, grand thoughts of perfection and greatness will one day materialize them. Einstein cherished his vision of laws of physics , and he discovered them; Edison envisioned bringing a source of light for everyday usage and after more than a hundred attempts, made the light bulbs reality ; 3,00 years back, Buddha had his vision of a spiritual world of enlightened existence and perfect peace, and he evolved into it.

 Pursue your lofty dreams ,cherish your visions; respect your ideals; develop and play out the music that stirs your heart and soul , the magnificence that forms in your mind, the beauty and loveliness that shapes your purest thoughts, because out of them will manifest ongoing wonderful reality, every set of heavenly experiences. Persist and persevere by keeping your efforts going and you will manifest noble ideals.

Conceive, believe and achieve is a law of the Universe . The measure of whether we can achieve lofty goals is not whether they are too lofty or kept low, the reality is whether we pursue them consistently with efforts and whether we keep our doubts and speculation out of the way and allow ourselves to reach out and achieve them.

Dream lofty dreams, and as you dream, so shall you become. Your Vision is the promise of what you shall one day be; your Ideal is the prophecy of what you shall at last unveil.

The greatest achievement was at first and for a time a dream. The oak sleeps in the acorn; the bird waits in the egg; and in the highest vision of the soul a waking angel stirs. Dreams are the seedlings of realities.

 a larger scope takes possession of him; unrest urges him to action, and he utilizes all his spare time and means, small though they are, to the development of his latent powers and resources. Very soon so altered has his mind become that the workshop can no longer hold him. It has become so out of harmony with his mentality that it falls out of his life as a garment is cast aside, and, with the growth of opportunities, which fit the scope of his expanding powers, he passes out of it forever. Years later we see this youth as a full-grown man. We find him a master of certain forces of the mind, which he wields with worldwide influence and almost unequaled power. In his hands he holds the cords of gigantic accounts, and presently you shall walk out of the door that for so long has seemed to you the barrier of your ideals, and shall find yourself before an audience--the pen still behind your ear, the ink stains on your fingers and then and there shall pour out the torrent of your inspiration. You may be driving sheep, and you shall wander to the city-bucolic and open-mouthed; shall wander under the intrepid guidance of the spirit into the studio of the master, and after a time he shall say, 'I have nothing more to teach you.' And now you have become the master, who did so recently dream of great things while driving sheep. You shall lay down the saw and the plane to take upon yourself the regeneration of the world."

The thoughtless, the ignorant, and the indolent, seeing only the apparent effects of things and not the things themselves, talk of luck, of fortune, and chance. Seeing a man grow rich, they say, "How lucky he is!" Observing another become intellectual, they exclaim, "How highly favored he is!" And noting the saintly character and wide influence of another, they remark, "How chance aids him at every turn!" They do not see the trials and failures and struggles which these men have voluntarily met to gain their experience; have no knowledge of the sacrifices they have made, of the undaunted efforts they have put forth, of the faith they have exercised, that they might overcome the apparently insurmountable, and realize the Vision of their heart. They do not know the darkness and the heartaches; they only see the light and joy, and call it "luck". They do not see the long and arduous journey, but only behold the pleasant goal, and call it "good fortune," do not understand the process, but only perceive the result, and call it chance.

In all human affairs there are efforts, and there are results, and the strength of the effort is the measure of the result. Chance is not. Gifts, powers, material, intellectual, and spiritual possessions are the fruits of effort; they are thoughts completed, objects accomplished, visions realized.

The Vision that you glorify in your mind, the Ideal

that you enthrone in your heart--this you will build your life by, this you will become.

Practice makes perfect. To keep inspired and motivated, to refer to what other authoritative people say on the subject, are listed here :

of mind is one of the beautiful jewels of wisdom. It is the result of long and patient effort in self-control. Its presence is an indication of ripened experience, and of a more than ordinary knowledge of the laws and operations of thought.

You become calm to the extent that you understand yourself as a thoughtful evolved being, for such knowledge necessitates the understanding of others as the result of thought, and as you develop the right understanding, and see more and more clearly the internal relations of things by the action of cause and effect you stop to fuss and fume and worry and grieve, and remains poised, steadfast, serene. That's the state of perfect harmony between the body, mind and spirit- keep that focus on serenity and you will state in that ideal state of harmony more and more

The calm man, having learned how to govern

himself, knows how to adapt himself to others; and they, in turn, reverence his spiritual strength, and feel that they can learn of him and rely upon him. The more tranquil a man becomes, the greater is his success, his influence, his power for good. Even the ordinary trader will find his business prosperity increase as he develops a greater self-control and equanimity, for people will always prefer to deal with a man whose demeanor is strongly equable.

The strong, calm man is always loved and revered. He is like a shade-giving tree in a thirsty land, or a sheltering rock in a storm. "Who does not love a tranquil heart, a sweet-tempered, balanced life? It does not matter whether it rains or shines, or what changes come to those possessing these blessings, for they are always sweet, serene, and calm. That exquisite poise of character, which we call serenity is the last lesson of culture, the fruit age of the soul. It is precious as wisdom, more to be desired than gold--yea, than even fine gold. How insignificant mere money seeking looks in comparison with a serene life--a life that dwells in the ocean of truth, beneath the waves, beyond the reach of tempests, in the eternal calm!

"How many people we know who sour their lives, who ruin all that is sweet and beautiful by explosive tempers, who destroy their poise of character, and make bad blood! It is a question whether the great majority of people do not ruin their lives and mar their happiness by lack of self-control. How few people we meet in life who are well balanced, who have that exquisite poise which is characteristic of the finished character!

Positive thinking and the power of optimism are the foundation for better and fulfilled living.

If you want to make changes in your life, you must look to the causes, and the causes are almost always the way you are using your mind — the way you are thinking. You cannot think both negative and positive thoughts at the same time. One or the other will dominate. The mind is a creature of habit, so it becomes each individual's responsibility to make sure that positive emotions and thoughts constitute the dominating influence in their mind.

In order to change external conditions, you must first change the internal. Most people omit this step. They try to change external conditions by working directly on those conditions. This always proves futile, or at best temporary, unless it is accompanied by a change of thoughts and beliefs.

Awakening to this truth, the way to a better, more successful life becomes crystal clear. Train your conscious mind to think thoughts of success, happiness, health, prosperity, and to weed out negativity such as fear and worry. Keep your conscious mind busy with the expectation of the best, and make sure the thoughts you habitually think are based upon what you want to see happen in your life. Water takes the shape of whatever container holds it, whether it be in a glass, a vase or a riverbank. Likewise, your mind will create and manifest according to the images you habitually think about in your daily thinking. This is how your destiny is created. A new life is created by new thoughts.

We have much to be grateful for here at unlimited opportunity to share the love, knowledge and understanding that we have received, with you. Together we can make a positive impact on the whole world.

When we know ourselves, we know that everything in existence is love expressing intelligently through energy. We are that and so is everyone and everything else. Separateness is only in form. We see energy manifested in different forms. These forms are created by thought. We believe that we are separate because we are not aware of our wholeness.

All of this awareness and experience is available to us through the development of our right brain abilities. When we begin to work with a process for releasing stress and strengthening or refining our nervous systems, we begin to discover who we are on a deeper level and soon begin to know the wholeness that includes all of us and everything else in existence. When this happens we begin to understand that all aspects of life are governed by laws of nature or principles of life, and we start to see what these principles are, and how they work. At this point we move into a much more advanced level of functioning, and discover that we have the power right within ourselves to create whatever we choose.

Adopt these specific ways for empowering yourself as a daily, consistent practice. For all of us there is always a higher plane of evolution and fulfillment. There is always one more notch to improve further towards enlightenment. Use these simple techniques to activate your mind to higher planes:

a. Trust the Universe: Remind and commit yourself to accept the highest energies and the greater good of the Universe.

b. Release negativity : Internalize and repeat this statement at regular intervals during the day:" I am willing to release all negative patterns in my consciousness by wrapping them with love and letting them float far,far, far away into nothingness."

b Forgive : the process of forgiveness is more

than forgetting the past to move into the present, it is for building growing peace within yourself through regular repetition of ::" I forgive myself and all others, everybody also forgives me for everything in all dimensions of time and space. I am released , totally free and in peace.

c. Visualizations

d. Affirmations

So, what keeps you all trapped in your current 3D context is your continuous clinging"to outcomes (cause and effect relationships) that you imagine are

operation there. These are mere illusions.

When something manifests in your 3D world, it arrives because you *called for it* with your mind and heart. t makes little difference whether your call was a conscious one, or whether it was something that as issued from beneath your veil of forgetfulness. It came from you, and you need to own that before you can break free from its influence. hose who have trouble with this concept may need to circle back

A person doesn't manifest his or her world out of woolgathering,each of you forms your personal reality from the everything, which exists all around you. In order to make something physical, you simply focus upon it.....(which slows down the vibration sufficiently for it to solidify), and then you install perceptual veils around it, to block Mouthe awareness of everything else that is there. This is your own perceptual equivalent of putting blinders on a horse.

As you begin your process of focusing, you must clearly realize how the creative element of your mind works. T he explanation we are going to make for you now is a linear one,because you are currently operating within a linear reality base. Please realize that you have the power to change the order or the rules of this process at any time.

Your affirmative statements, especially when accompanied by true desire and passion, are like Genies from a bottle, granting you everything you could ever wish for. As one Spiritual master once phrased it: "The universe rearranges itself according to your beliefs about what is real." It does this through your own declarations of *what is,* not through declarations of *what is not.

You must realize that physical reality is created from focus. f you are constantly focusing upon what

Here is a step-wise practice which will be most effective when practiced twice a day for at least thirty days. Z Try to do it over 30 consecutive days , but if you miss a day or two in between, catch up with the count as soon as you can

Settle yourself in a quiet space getting away from all activities and start by breathing in and out slow and deep, taking in imagined , pure divine energy and exhaling all negative patterns, tension and strain from your body.

Let go of all thoughts, feelings...and just allow yourself to relax.

As you continue to breathe deeply, slowly direct your attention to your heart ,

pause, pause and stay drifting in your relaxed

state.

Second step:Clearly state your wish in a sentence or two, regardless of how ambitious or outlandish your wish may seem at that time

 Now,imagine God has just appeared above you and grants you three wishes. Anything you want!

What are your three wishes? (go to your heart and let your heart choose your deepest desire)

If you could only have one wish, which wish would you choose? Remember you must choose only one!

 Hint: Select something you want, not something your want to get rid of.

For Example: If my last want is to be healthy and one of the ways for me to be healthy is to lose weight

my choice would read like this: I choose to be healthy and physically fit. Rather than I want to lose weight.

 Clearly state your deepest desire. It is helpful to write it down where you can see it daily.

Step Three: Visualize Success In Advance
 Picture what you desire as if it has already

happened,

as if it has already manifested for you in your life.

Allow your picture to be as vivid as possible...colorful, life like, real

Step Four: Embrace The Feeling

What feeling will having your desire give you?

Feel the feeling you have as you imagine having your desire now.

Hint: Let's use the example of I desire more money in my life. Ask yourself what feeling do you have as you

imagine having all the money you desire? Perhaps you feel rich, wealthy, secure, successful, relieved. Beyond

these feelings, what do you feel? Most people report a deeper feeling of peace, freedom. The deeper feeling is

what you want to feel. This is known as your core value.

Step Five: Create An Image

Allow an image to come to you that represents your core feeling.

The image can be a place, a person, an object, a color, a shape

Hint: If your core feeling is freedom, an image that may work would be a bird,

sailing on the ocean, parasailing, space. If your core feeling is peace an image may

be a sunset, a dove, walking in nature, the color pink, Mother Theresa, a rose.

Step Six: Let It Go!

Let your mind release the intention to your higher self.

Hint: This can be done by merely saying to yourself " I now release my

desire to the wisdom and power of my higher self." And allow your mind to shift

to your core feeling. As you energize your core feeling, you will manifest your desires

ten fold.

Step Seven: Have faith

Have faith that you have done all that needs to be done.

Your higher self, Your subconscious mind will handle the rest.

 I suggest you use these steps every day. Taking a few minutes in the morning when you first

awaken is an excellent time to take yourself through these seven steps.

Once you become

familiar with these steps, you will be able to do them quickly, without needing to write them down.

 Feel free to use these steps during your day as well. It is an excellent way to keep yourself focused on

what is most important to you.

CHAPTER NINE

Many studies have shown that making daily lists of the things you feel grateful for—which helps draw our attention to the positive happenings in your lives—improves our psychological and physical health and well-being. For example, gratitude improves our ability to connect with others, boosts our compassionate expressions make us optimistic and happier, decreases envy and materialism and even improves health for people with physical ailments (bone related accidents in two patients). however, extends studies on gratitude to show that verbally expressing the gratitude we feel to people close to us helps increase and sustain our well-being above and beyond simply feeling or writing down gratitude. Great literary figures have

The experts found that people who habitually tend to talk to people they are close with about the good things that are happening to them also tend to feel happier and more satisfied with life. They also found that, the more these people shared their joyfulness with someone on a given day, the happier and more satisfied they were on that day. To determine whether sharing joyfulness caused this boost in well-being, the experts then invited into a laboratory with a romantic companion or friend. were asked to write down a positive experience or a neutral experience like a fact they had learned in class and either share it with their companion or not. Those that shared a positive experience with their companion experienced a greater boost in well-being than those who did not share their experience with their companion or who shared a neutral experience with their companion. These findings suggest that it is the act of sharing joyfulness (and not of just thinking about joyfulness but not sharing it, or of sharing neutral information) that boosts well being.

they felt grateful for, or about neutral subjects they had learned in class. They were then either given no further instructions or were instructed to share these with a companion twice a week. Those who shared their grateful happenings with a companion reported greater satisfaction with life, joyfulness and vitality (level of energy and for life).

One reason that the study asked to share their experience with close friends or these people may be more likely to support us. The process of discovering , enhancing and spreading joy has very beneficial, far-reaching effects. After getting benefited ourselves with health and happiness joy spreads out to reach other people linked to us unto three degrees of connections.(which is each of our close friend's friend's friends) thus encompassing a wide social group. The beneficial effects are further compounded when other appreciative, like-minded people in our social circle also do the discovery, enhancement and spreading process which in turn radially spreads out to their three degrees of connections. It is however important to select people who are appreciative and supportive of each of our efforts because they become strong links in spreading joy to an entire community which can benefit from the efforts of several people.

To sum up: sharing our joy increases joy. Telling people about our joyfulness has far greater benefits than just remembering it or writing it down for ourselves. those around turn, we can help support others' joy by encouraging them to share their most positive happenings, and the things they feel grateful for. Supporting a friend or acquaintance's well-being in turn may impact not only ourselves but the well-being of all the people

CHAPTER TEN

50 WAYS TO ENHANCE POSITIVE THINKING

Life is a mixed bag. There are patches when everything works in our favor. Other times, it is a wonderful morning mixed with a challenge in the evening. Weeks and months of happy events at a stretch, then suddenly some mistakes or an accident, which makes us unbalanced a bit ; to stay calm and composed, regardless of what happens, remind yourself to react with peaceful responses to the assortment of good, mediocre and bad happenings.

off track, but remember that most extenuating circumstances are temporary. Gain more clarity by staying the course and channeling your energy in a positive direction.

2. Trust yourself. Believe in your inner resources, no matter what, and you'll grow from the experience. I believe that the answers usually lie within and you are probably smart enough to figure out what you need to do. Give yourself a little time and have patience.

3. Once in a month or so, take ten to 15 minutes off in solitude to do some mental cleansing. Here are three tips to go over mentally during such quiet time: a) Forgive and be forgiven by saying- I forgive myself for everything, in all spaces and time, I forgive everybody for everything and everybody forgives me. Now I am released and free and at peace. Second:I am willing to release all negative patterns within me, wrap them within love and let all negative patterns vanish forever"

4. Watch your thoughts. Your thinking will never be 100 percent positive. You must learn to dismiss the negative thoughts and stay open to other ideas that will help you move in a positive direction. Start recognizing negative thoughts and use your mind to quell them.

5. Believe that you are complete in every way: Learn to access and direct your energy towards the highest good for all concerned. Believe that your innate intelligence and capabilities can help you deal with anything. Self-confidence and high self-worth are important components for happy, fulfilled living.

6. Learn to love yourself. You do not have to be who you are today, and your life is not scripted. Changing how you feel about yourself means creating a strategy, gathering some new tools, and making yourself into the person you want to be. A good way to start is to stop doing things that hurt.

7.Temper your greed. To get to own many things can be a propelling motivation for effort, however being greedy so keep levelheaded and aim for achieving good things without getting unbalanced Maintain moral and ethical norms for going after all that you desire.

8.Accept criticism in a cal and balanced way. It is smart to be dispassionate about critical comments.

 Recognize that disappointment is part of life. Even the most successful people must deal with disappointment, but they've learned how to use it to get to the next level of life. The trick is to process your feelings, then act

10. Deal with your hesitancy. Overcoming hesitancy makes you stronger, and being a little

scared can make you better. You want to have butterflies; you just want them flying in formation. It helps to understand and admit your hesitancy. Then you can kick them to the curb.

Increase your Joy today-wherever and whoever you are. Start with these:

1.Deep breathing outdoors: Step outdoors, take in the wide, open vistas, appreciate the bounty of nature and do slow, deep breathing (As you breathe in, visualize taking in pure, white, radiant light of the Universe in and imagine it reinvigorating your entire body and mind. As you breathe out, imagine exhaling from within all toxins and bitterness out of your system . Make this a habit whenever and wherever you have access to natural outdoor surroundings. Oxygen intake and the slow , deliberate pace of breathing will do away with your stress and bring your body and mind to an energetic, joyous state.

2.Keep that smile on: Practice smiling, as if you are pleased with yourself and all that is going on in your life. To become joyous, the biggest rule is : Act Joyous The initial make belief smile will start giving you enough reasons to be happy about. Whenever you can remember to switch them on, keep on repeating silently to yourself: I am the goodness of the Universe and I am grateful for it right now and at all times.

3. Ten minute walking: Being a lot on the

computers or electronic devices, most of us tend to skip the basic exercise that will be helpful for our well being. Remind yourself and follow up everyday to walk for at least ten minutes at a stretch. Whenever and wherever you can fit 10 continuous minutes of walking, enjoy that time exclusively for enjoying the exhilarating feeling of your body moving in purposeful strides. This will give your whole body a good workout, get all your body cells in a feel good condition and put you in a joyful state of mind.

4. Enjoy yourself and relish food and mealtimes: whether it is hurried breakfast time or a snack or a meeting over lunch or the dinner with a drink, maintain two common factors always -relish what you eat and be grateful for the food you are eating. These are relatively easy to do and work wonders for maintaining your physical and mental energy levels and regenerating joy when you affirm gratitude for good food.

5.Take a break from the routine, work from a new location, do your reading or work on the computer from a different location or outdoors, maybe even from a WI-fi wired café, getting away from the routine, reducing the routine boredom factor will bring in spurts of joy.

6..Listen to songs- Most of us can access songs sources and can use devices to listen to songs of our choice. If you don't have a specific choice or like several genres, switch between several types and experiment and enjoy what hits your fancy and gets you humming.

7 . Spend time with positive people while working and/or during leisure hours. Positive thinking sends out healthy and uplifting impulses to trillions of your mind and body cells, shifting you to a joyful mood.

8. Positive Affirmations-perhaps the easiest, fastest and absolutely free joyful magical application. Start with simple steps and build this into a continuous habit: keep repeating in your mind , in the present tense, that you are joy, joyfulness, goodness, well-being, health, prosperity

9. Play with or groom your pet

10. Maintain regular sleep times- go for 7 to 8 hours a sleep every night- a good night's sleep is the best way to recharge our mind and body cells and awaken fresh in the morning, re-affirm , to yourself, that you are happy, healthy, joyous and receiving abundance of good things in life.

11. No complaining:Stop yourself,every time you find yourself or you feel you may start like complaining- in many situations,either there is an option out , like if he room feels a bit cold or a bit hot, you can fix it by walking around or stepping out for a while to feel better. However, if its raining in sheets of water or snowing with multiple

inches on the ground, grant it to severe weather and make the most of the indoors. A single complaint can perpetuate complaining, so without feeling sorry for yourself , find a way out of inconvenient situations and make the best of all circumstances. 12.Meditation-There are several techniques of meditation and meditation has countless benefits endless, but perhaps one of the more positive perks is what the practice can do for your mood. studies shows that allowing yourself a few moments of zen-like escape each day may make you joyful.

12. Law of attraction: Several approaches to this- visualize with as much clarity and detail your ideal, happy image and what you want your life to be; just keep doing this in an enjoyable, light-heated way because feeling tense and over-anxious doesn't work. Secondly, keep in mind that you will attract to yourself how you think about yourself, so think being creative and gifted, attractive, accomplished, working in fun circumstances and enjoying things and company of people which you would like to keep. You could change images in your mind as you go along and having defined the ideal set of circumstances, let go of them and let the Universe work out the details on the path you have to follow to get what you want.

13.Help others, donate your time and money to those who need or ask for

What goes around, comes around. Our efforts to help others make others happy and gives us satisfaction and joyfulness. By the law of karma, help to others is rewarded by somebody helping us Not only will your kindness influence others, studies show it'll also make you happier, too.

14Spend time with happy , positive thinking people

Joy is really contagious. studies shows the more you surround yourself with positive people, the happier you'll feel.

15.Planning fun events , activities and outings:

16 Lightheartedness , laughter and rejoicing: Each of these are priceless traits to be cultivated using tools like sports, hobbies, plays, theater, music and social media networking.

17.Live in the present: Although planning ahead and scheduling our activities are essential for best utilizing our time to accomplish personal and professional goals, font let doubts and apprehensions come in the way of living in the moment and enjoying every bit of fun and fulfillment.

18..Have fun exercising:

. Not only is it good for your body, but it's equally as beneficial to your brain. When you work up a sweat, you release endorphins, immediately raising your joyfulness levels. Go ahead, get moving.

19.Spend money on happenings.

A fulfilling life doesn't lie in our possessions, it's found in the happenings we have and the people we share them with. If you're going to spend some money, spend it on a trip, a concert or any other experience that will bring you joy. Science says you'll be happier in the long run.

20. Challenge yourself.

Work for that promotion or take on that marathon. It's a lovely treat for your mind, according to Gretchen Rubin, author of The joyfulness Project. "Challenge and novelty are key elements of joyfulness," Rubin wrote in Real Simple. "The brain is stimulated by surprise, and successfully dealing with an unexpected situation gives a powerful sense of satisfaction."

21. Smiling

Make believe that somebody is taking your photograph. Put on your best , smile as many times a day you as you get aware that smiling is beneficial. If the smile doesn;t come on easily, think of any joke you shared with friends-recalling moments which were lighthearted, playful, spontaneous may make you chuckle, the very least they will help you put on a smile for yourself. Psychologists confirm that just by faking smiles many times during the day, help stretch facial and neck muscles and relieve stress. With spontaneous smiling, we can elevate our moods, become lighthearted enough to share and appreciate the lighter side of life and keep our mood uplifted.

22.Enjoy the outdoors.

Take advantage of your backyard or stroll a park you've never been to before and thank yourself later. One study found that going for a brief walk in nature can help improve your mood and alleviate stress.

23.Make some new friends.

studies shows making friends increases our joyfulness and well-being. Join a club, talk to your coworker or strike up a conversation in the grocery line — you never know what kinds of new connections you can make.
24.. Drink a glass of milk.

Dairy contains Aristophanes, an essential amino acid that helps create serotonin, the "happy" chemical in the brain. Milk: It not only does the body good, it does the brain good too.

25..Keep in close touch with nature

Feel the simple joy of walking barefoot on clean, freshly mowed grass or get the tingling feeling of walking on clean sand during a stroll along the beach. Take in the fresh air and the calm as you listen to the sounds of nature. Enjoying the beauty of nature in most panoramas, landscapes and formations is the best prescription for relieving boredom, stress, cynicism. Access to nature is easy , free and in abundance, so go enjoy nature as much as you can. Take some friend or pet along too and experience the euphoria of freedom, joyousness, well-being and vitality surge into you.

26.Doze off for short power naps once in a while.

While safely on a train ride home or during lunch time on the park bench, doze off for ten minutes or so. You will be amazed with the refreshed rejuvenated self and the wonders of doing away with fatigue and stress as you wake up with a clear mind and energy surplus for the rest of the day.

 slows down our cognitive processes and increases the risk of depression. Try hitting the pillow 30 minutes earlier each night or taking a nap in the middle of the day.

27..Celebrate milestones-big or small.

28 Compliment others: One of the simplest forms of feeling good is to complement others and appreciate something about what they do:

29.Positive talk at the mirror

30.Meditation

Subscribe to The Good Life email.

No moon dust. No B.S. Just a completely essential daily guide to achieving the good life.

31.Give someone else a compliment.

Your generosity will make your day and theirs. Looking for a way to give praise that isn't superficial? Here are some ideas.

32. Find the perfect temperature.

The weather outside has a direct influence on how we feel on the inside. One study found that joyfulness is maximized at an approximate 57 degrees Fahrenheit.

33.Keep a one-sentence private diary.

Sometimes the most mundane moments turn out to be the loveliest source of joyfulness. studies shows recording these everyday events may make us happier later on because we appreciate them a lot more when they're revisited. In other words, if you ate a scrumptious chocolate brownie on Wednesday, write it down.

34.Stop to smell the flowers, literally.

One study on how scent affects joy found that who were in a floral-scented room selected three times as many joyfulness-related terms than negative terms.

35.Lots of safe, pleasurable sex.

A good way to express your fun, passionate, playful, creative personality. Sexologists confirm that there is no minimum, average or maximum number of times or length of time-different people have different norms, routines and opportunities but good, clean, pleasurable,caring, sharing sexual encounters relax the body and mind, lift the spirits and help enhance health and happiness.

36.Plan interesting events: Weekends and holidays are perfect for doing fun things.plan to go discover some park, a hiking trail, pond or stream or the beach. Check out the weather forecast, the best way to reach your destination,what to wear and things to pack. Include some like -minded person ,if available. Looking forward to and later enjoying fun activities is inherently relaxing and produces body hormones that make us happy, lighthearted and rejuvenated.

37.. Release stress: you can begin anywhere and with any simple pastime- a dartboard, punching bag, skipping rope, tossing a smurf ball or a balloon. You may find advanced methods interesting as well- yoga, Pilates, meditation. Have fun with whatever you experiment with or pick up long-term and surprise your family or friends with a friendlier, relaxed, happier you.

38.Praying

At times when life seems difficult and future outcomes seem uncertain, many of us turn to praying for things to work out well. Ever since the dawn of civilization, humans have turned their eyes and minds upwards to the Cosmos to grant them their wishes. Simply stated, prayers have worked for billions and they give confidence to the seeker that things will improve. Whatever our personal religious beliefs, there is evidence that prayers can improve our well being, health and joyfulness and help achieve many tangibles and intangibles.

39.Forgiveness: The act of forgiving oneself and forgiving others helps ourselves detach from remorse and grudges that have lingered on in our subconscious, although events have been long past over. Unless we get rid of the baggage that many of us carry around for long, we will be unable to work fully on improving our health and joyfulness. It is very important to forgive ourselves and others for everything with conscious spoken intentions. After forgiving everybody and everything , it is best to conclude the forgiving process by accepting that we are free and released and we are at peace.

40.Releasing bitterness: Most of us have read about, experienced and learn that adopting positive thinking acts as a catalyst towards achieving our goals, dreams and desires. The additional factor about this is to release bitterness , which many of us have unknowingly embedded in our subconscious. Time for some spring cleaning to eject negative patterns sunk in mostly subconscious levels. This is best done in solitude with very specific spoken and written intentions that you are releasing all negative patterns from deep within and letting them go far away into nothingness. You guessed it, you will after some sessions start feeling crystal clear and clean and that's when you can start with inviting positive thoughts and positive belief paternoster your conscious and subconscious mind.

41.. Art supplies

pick up some art supplies: art paper, crayons, paper painting set and make time for 5/10 minutes for sketching/coloring whatever comes to you as natural inspiration-the sun, car, a human , dog , cat, clouds or a pond or boat , maybe a single flower. This simple activity will start your creative juices flowing and get you in a relaxed, happy state of mind.40 percent of us take to sketching and art as a hobby well into adulthood and most of them reported to studies that they had reduced minor ailments as migraines, heartburn and high blood pressure levels

42..Repeat positive affirmations to yourself.

You can either create your own positive affirmations or find some online (personally, we like these encouraging words). Search for a phrase that's going to bring meaning to you. studies shows having a mantra can help with bad feelings. Find yours!

43.Love your self:Loving oneself is not getting on an ego trip, but it's mainly taking care of oneself, being gentle and kind and building up self-worth , which is an inherent evaluation about what we are worth and how much we deserve in our personal and professional lives. Be gentle , kind and loving to yourself, with no remorse or feelings of guilt and no regrets anytime. Whatever we have done and will do at all times and places was best at that moment of time with the information, aptitude and resources we have available under the circumstances. Moreover, we can only love others after we start and keep loving ourselves.

44 Love what you do and do what you love: many of us have evaluated several options and are doing what we love and what suits us most. If you are stuck in a dead-end job or career, seek options and opportunities to switch when the time comes, but loving what you are doing at the moment will give you satisfaction about your commitment and work value system.

45.Walking ten minutes everyday- loosen up your muscles and joints and feel the joy as your organs function optimally Walking releases endorphins into your blood stream and make you feel joyful and energetic. Its more than what the doctor ordered, it's a refreshing way to have fun too.

The next time someone judges you for taking one of those infamous front-facing photos, show them this: A 2016 study found that selfies actually increase confidence and make you happier.

46.Meeting new, like-minded people: Get personal, beyond phone calls, texts and e-mails and meet new, like-minded people. Getting, giving and sharing new perspectives is refreshing-many times joyous and results in healthy living. Research studies shows we simply feel better when we're around lively, positive other people.

47.Power of prayers:Whatever your heritage, community or faith and whatever name you grant God:creator of the universe, the Supreme Being, God,Universe Divinity, Spirit, in moments of need and as a regular practice reach out and ask for what you seek and ask for help in the form of prayers..Millions have asked for and received help. Believe in the power of prayer and to those who pray regularly, their faith reinforces that nothing will be denied. Prayers are the surest ways for discovering and increasing joy and for healthy, happy living.

48.Positive Thinking, Power of Optimism

If you think you can, you will. If you think you cant, you wont. Go for the things that you want with a positive attitude and celebrate on receiving all things you focus on. lining in any situation. Optimists are not only more joyful, they also may live longer. That's a lot of extra time to be happy.

49. Hum for 30 seconds any of your favorite, happy songs You will instantly feel a joyous uplift. Try to make this a habit, by remembering few songs that make you feel good and hum these as and when you get chance. Keep that momentum going for keeping lighthearted, happy and confident using as many ways as you have learned.

50. Have faith in Divinity: this point underlines everything you do in life .You are aliveandblessed with many tangible and intangible things. Divinity has brought you intact so far in your life, so trust in Spirit to help you continue forward and sustain your joy and well-being.

These are numerous , independent resources which you may find useful in your ongoing steps towards

self-improvement..

Disclaimer: you will do your own research to learn more about these and rely on and use them at your own discretion and your own risk based on your individual situation

https://www.dmoz.org/Health/Mental_Health/Self-Help/

https://www.dmoz.org/Society/Religion_and_S
pirituality/New_Age/Magazines_and_E-zines/

ABOUT THE AUTHOR

Positive Thinking Mentor&Author Gautam Sharma (an intelligent, accomplished, capable,creative professional) was born in India, has lived in Asia, Europe, Africa and now living in USA embodies and edifies positive thinking power of optimism and is sharing insights into human behavior and human potential through philosophical, psychological perspectives with the view of sharing mankind's centuries-old wisdom plus proven, research findings so as to empower people worldwide. The author plans to utilize his strengths of professionalism,wide,varied experiences , creativity and communications' skills to publish the Empowerment Series on improvement, self help topics. Thank you valued readers for your continuous support , contributions and your favorable feedback. Wishing everybody abundance of positive thinking and better living through the power of optimism.

OTHER BOOKS BY THE AUTHOR , GAUTAM SHARMA

Self Confidence Self Esteem for Happiness and Success

https://www.amazon.com/SELF-CONFIDENCE-ESTEEM-HAPPINESS-SUCCESS-ebook/dp/B076VM1MNR/ref=tmm_kin_swatch_0?
_encoding=UTF8&qid=1514483766&sr=1-1

and JOY FOR HEALTHY , HAPPY LIVING

 https://www.amazon.com/JOY-forHEALTHY-HAPPY-LIVING-Empowerment-ebook/dp/B078L6Y1YM/ref=sr_1_1?s=digital-text&ie=UTF8&qid=1514484176&sr=1-1

www.ingramcontent.com/pod-product-compliance
Lightning Source LLC
Chambersburg PA
CBHW062008280526
45787CB00005B/2026